# Doing Dissertations in Politics

This guide has been designed to help undergraduates develop an understanding of practical research methods and their application in preparing the undergraduate dissertation. Written in an accessible and engaging style, it offers advice on all aspects of undergraduate research, from choosing a dissertation subject through to presenting the finished article.

Features of this book:

- Concise chapters providing introductions to various aspects of research methods, including: why they are important, quantitative and qualitative methods, and their practical application.
- Advice, hints and tips on planning, presenting, researching and writing undergraduate dissertations.
- A wide range of examples of research to clearly illustrate different issues and methods which students may encounter.
- A dedicated website containing useful links and discussion questions to test your knowledge: <http://www.routledge. com/textbooks/doingdissertations.html>.

**David M. Silbergh** teaches Research Methods at The Robert Gordon University, Aberdeen, UK.

David M.
# Silbergh

# Doing dissertations in politics

A student guide

 London and New York

First published 2001
by Routledge
11 New Fetter Lane, London EC4P 4EE

Simultaneously published in the USA and Canada
by Routledge
29 West 35th Street, New York, NY 10001

*Routledge is an imprint of the Taylor & Francis Group*

Typeset in Joanna by RefineCatch Limited, Bungay, Suffolk
Printed and bound in Great Britain by
TJ International Ltd, Padstow, Cornwall

*British Library Cataloguing in Publication Data*
A catalogue record for this book is available from the British Library

*Library of Congress Cataloging in Publication Data*
Sibergh, David M.,
    Doing dissertations in politics : a student guide / David M. Silbergh.
        p.   cm.
    Includes bibliographical references and index.
    1. Political science—Research—Handbooks, manuals, etc.
    2. Political science—Methodology—Handbooks, manuals, etc.
    3. Dissertations, Academic—Handbooks, manuals, etc.   I. Title.
JA86 .S55   2001
808'.06632—dc21                                        2001019496

ISBN 0–415–24685–7 (hbk)
ISBN 0–415–24686–5 (pbk)

# DEDICATION

For Sandy, Anne and Mylae Silbergh. My parents, my wife.

# CONTENTS

# ILLUSTRATIONS

## PLATES

A political problem

## FIGURES

## TABLES

# PREFACE

Most of the literature available for students to draw upon when researching and writing their undergraduate dissertation in politics has not been written with them in mind. For example, most of the texts available have been written from a sociological or psychological perspective. The end result of this is often confusion on the part of the student, who is inevitably faced with examples that are not of relevance and extended commentary on methods that are unlikely to prove of practical use in their own dissertation research. Moreover, many of the texts available address the needs of postgraduate as opposed to undergraduate students, yet the requirements of the undergraduate and the postgraduate dissertation are clearly not one and the same.

It is for these reasons that this book was written, to try to redress the balance in favour of the undergraduate student of politics. The book is compact and consequently cannot cover everything. This is entirely intentional. There are many excellent books covering the detailed aspects of this or that method of research and throughout this volume students will be directed to them as appropriate. Thus, the purpose of this book is not to produce specialised methodologists, but is to provide a rounded introduction to the process of producing a high quality undergraduate dissertation in politics. In terms of using the book, the reader is encouraged to read it at least once in its entirety before starting work on their dissertation. It can then be 'dipped into' as and when required as work progresses.

DS, Aberdeen, 2001

# ACKNOWLEDGEMENTS

In preparing this book I have drawn upon the rich educational experiences that I have been fortunate enough to enjoy throughout my life thus far. I am therefore, deeply indebted to all those from whom I have learned both within and without the formal education system. Foremost in my mind are the three people to whom this book is dedicated, but there are many others, too numerous to mention individually. I do however wish to express heartfelt thanks to the staff of both Cluny Primary and Buckie High Schools, as I cannot remember having ever taken the opportunity to thank them properly for the professional but unfortunately often unrecognised job that they do.

Furthermore, there are a number of colleagues, past and present, to whom I am more indebted than they may realise. They are as follows: Prof. Seaton Baxter OBE; Ms Nicole Busby; Prof. Jan Magnus Fladmark; Dr Calum Macleod; Prof. Alistair McCulloch; Mr John Moxen; Mrs Anne Simpson; and the late Dr Keith Maguire. The continued unconditional support and encouragement of these people has been absolutely vital to the realisation of this and many other projects.

I cannot of course do anything other than record my sincere gratitude to Mark Kavanagh, editor at Routledge, who is the man responsible for this book seeing the light of day. He has been positive about this work since we first spoke about it and throughout the processes of writing, editing and production he has shown himself to be a model professional. His encouragement, advice and patience have been truly appreciated. Mr Bill Black also deserves thanks as he kindly gave of his time to take the photographs for the plates (in between chasing cats round his studio). Copyright of the photographs is jointly vested in him and the author.

Finally though, any errors found within this volume are the author's and his alone.

# A political problem

*Plate 1* As explained by theory A

*Plate 2* As found in the empirical world

*Plate 3* As explained by theory B

# 1

## DOING DISSERTATIONS IN POLITICS

### INTRODUCTION

More or less regardless of the educational system, at an advanced
level of your undergraduate studies you will be faced with the
prospect of writing a dissertation for the first time. Although
there can be a good deal of variation between what is expected
of a dissertation in different countries, at different institutions of
higher education and in different departments (not to mention
differing expectations on the part of tutors and examiners) there
are also a great many areas of commonality. It is across these
areas of commonality that this small volume will range. This
book will not be the only resource that you need to consult in
undertaking your dissertation studies. Hopefully though, it will
serve as a compact and handy source that can assist in guiding
you through what is, thus far at least, uncharted territory. Further basic reading has been suggested throughout the text in all
chapters and this serves to direct you to further relevant

materials as regards this subject or that. In a volume of this size it is evidently impossible to cover everything, but then it is also impossible to cover everything in a tome of 1,000 pages. Thus, the purpose of this book is primarily to direct the reader through the process of preparing a dissertation with reference to as wide a range of issues as space allows and with regard to both fundamental principles and practical advice. In other words, this volume will seek to address (albeit in a truncated fashion) both the dogmatic and pragmatic issues with which you should concern yourself in the preparation of a dissertation. Whatever else you take from the book, bear in mind that the process of doing a dissertation is mainly about striking the right balance between dogma and pragma. This can be achieved through nothing more spectacular than employing your own considered judgement, informed by the relevant literature and aided and abetted by the advice of your dissertation tutor. If you can get this balance and judgement right, it makes it much easier to then demonstrate to the outside world that you have taken full account of all the relevant issues (both dogmatic and pragmatic) in the final written piece. Put in another way, if you get the balance and judgement right, you should be able to produce a high quality dissertation.

A quality dissertation is something to be proud of. It may be the longest and most focused piece of academic work that you ever undertake and it will stay with you for the rest of your life. In an attainment sense (it will play an important part in determining your overall award classification) you can never get rid of it − it is an integral part of your degree parchment. In a physical sense you'll probably find that you're unlikely to ever part with it (although admittedly it may start off on top of the coffee table but end up propping it up some years down the line). Even if, like the author's, it ends up in some forgotton box in the attic you will, if you have pride in it, never forget its contents. The author hasn't looked at his own undergraduate dissertation for about a decade but can still share with you that it involved a comparative study of political and economic pressures and their respective influence on decision-making in the National Health Service in the North East of Scotland. Although this may sound boring and trivial (and maybe it is) what you will undoubtedly have to do if your dissertation is to be completed on time, to a high standard and with the minimum of fuss, is to have a sufficiently clear and focused problem to address at the outset. The author has personally seen too many dissertations that consist of general musings on 'The National Health Service in Britain: 1950–2000' and such like to know that the broad-brush approach just does not work. In the final analysis the dissertation is a focused piece of academic work that you are undertaking as part of your degree studies. If you desperately want to write a tome on 'Political Ideology: 2000 BC to 2000 AD' then you are of course free to do so; all that is being suggested here is that you should finish off a more realistic piece of work for your dissertation first.

Thus, if in discussing potential topics with your dissertation tutor they suggest that your focus is too broad and needs to be reined in somewhat, do take their advice. Although all decisions as to what your dissertation will and will not cover are undoubtedly yours and yours alone, do remember that your tutor has had more experience of dissertations than you. This is not a criticism, just an observation of a simple fact of life. One day you may well have more experience of dissertations than they do. In the meantime however, do listen carefully to their advice and take what they say to you seriously. You do not always have to follow the tutor's advice to the letter (nor would they expect you to do so), but it is always offered in good faith. We shall return to this point periodically throughout the book. Wherever you are likely to benefit from seeking advice from your dissertation tutor a note will be made to this effect. The first step in undertaking any research project however is not something that a tutor will be able to assist you with to any great extent however. First of all, you must decide what *you* think the world is like.

## WHAT IS THE WORLD LIKE?

Although your immediate reaction to the question above may well be, 'Haven't a clue,' each and every person does carry around with them in their own mind a view of what the world is like. The only problem (and one that afflicts the author as much as anyone else) is that we cannot usually express this view in a clear, consistent and coherent fashion. Indeed, there are very few people who can provide a clear exposition of their world-view that is free from contradictions. When people can do this we call them philosophers. Although it may not always seem so, we, the human species, have derived enormous benefits from the mental toil of the philosophers of the present as well as of ages past and this situation will undoubtedly persist for ages to come.

Philosophical thought underpins all scientific and social scientific investigation and political research is no different from any other type in this regard. When philosophers provide explanations of what the world is like, their explanations are then used (consciously or otherwise) to provide reference frameworks within which scholarly activity can take place. Most philosophical thinking on what the world is like can be classified as being associated with one of two main 'ontological' frameworks (where ontology is the study of the nature of existence itself), namely the holistic framework and the individualistic framework. Tom Campbell has noted that the difference between these two frameworks has caused, 'Perhaps the most fundamental and persistent difference between social theories' (Campbell 1981: 36).

Without going into too much detail about the holistic–individualistic dichotomy, definitions of these terms will be offered here, followed by a brief discussion of their implications for social scientific research. Individualism can be defined as an ontological stance that is based on the view that there is, 'a fixed and universal human nature, independent of the effects of social conditioning, which is the ultimate explanation for social life' (Campbell 1981: 9).

This perspective is clearly explained by Frank Parkin in his discussion of the individualistic ontological stance of Max Weber:

> Only the individual is capable of 'meaningful' social action. Weber says that it may often be useful, for certain purposes, to treat social groups or aggregates 'as if' they were individual beings. But this is nothing more than an allowable theoretical fiction . . . Collectivities cannot think, feel, perceive; only people can. To assume otherwise is to impute a spurious reality to what are in effect conceptual abstractions.
>
> (Parkin 1982: 17–18)

Holism on the other hand can be defined as an opposing onto-logical stance where the world is viewed as being made up of large-scale social systems that have an existence in their own right, that is, 'it is not people in aggregate who constitute such a totality. Just adding them up, so to speak, will tell you nothing about a social structure other than how many people are in it' (Doyal and Harris 1986: 164).

This perspective is further explained by Frisby and Sayer in their exposition of the holistic ontological stance of Emile Durkheim:

> Durkheim's claim is that the 'being', society, which is formed out of the association of individuals, is a whole – an object – distinct from and greater than the sum of its parts. It forms a specific order of reality with its own distinctive characteristics . . . These characteristics of society are not reducible to nor,

> therefore, explicable from those of its component elements – human individuals – taken in isolation. Society has emergent properties, that is, properties which do not derive from its elements considered independently of their combination, but which arise from and do not exist outwith that combination itself.
>
> (Frisby and Sayer 1986: 36)

In terms of shaping the manner in which humans have interpreted and understood the world down the millennia, the holistic–individualistic dichotomy has played a central part. To summarise, an individualistic perspective purports: that the world is primarily made of small units (e.g. individuals and families); that it is these small units which are important to an understanding of the world around us; and, that it is upon these small units that we should focus our scholarly activities. Conversely, the holistic perspective purports that the world should be viewed as consisting of large units (e.g. governments and social classes), that it is these large units which are important to our understanding of it and that it is upon these large units that we should focus our investigations. See Table 1.1 for a brief schematic representation of how both holistic and individualistic thinking has contributed to the shaping of subject areas, theories of society and political ideas.

Furthermore, the holistic–individualistic dichotomy also feeds through into the types of study that social scientific researchers undertake. For example, the study of large-scale problems is most easily achieved through the assessment of the patterns found in large data sets. Conversely, the study of small-scale problems is most easily achieved through analysing these problems in considerable depth to identify the nature of the underlying mechanisms causing them. We will return to this issue in Chapters 5 and 6. As regards further reading in the meantime (for those who are interested), please refer to the

*Table 1.1* The holistic–individualistic dichotomy and its effects

|  | *Holistic perspective* | *Individualistic perspective* |
| --- | --- | --- |
| *Subject areas* | Ecology and sociology both underpinned by holism. Subjects that focus on large-scale issues, e.g. societies, ecosystems | Psychology and economics (micro) both underpinned by individualism. Subject focus on the individual or small groups of individuals |
| *Theories of society* | See comment on Emile Durkheim in this chapter | See comment on Max Weber in this chapter |
| *Political ideas* | Left-wing political thought informed by holism. Focus on large-scale issues such as class tension, collective ownership, strength in unity, social inclusion | Right-wing political thought informed by individualism e.g. Margaret Thatcher's infamous comment about there being no such thing as society |

following sources, all of which give an easy-to-understand explanation of the individualistic and holistic views of the world: Bergström (1993); Bookchin (1990); Campbell (1981); Doyal and Harris (1986); Frisby and Sayer (1986).

## WHERE DOES POLITICS FIT?

Once we have figured out what we think the world is like in general, the next thing that we must do is recognise that it is so complex and filled with so many problems that we cannot address them all. This was not always so; for instance, the Ancient Greek philosophers would happily address issues of faith, ethics, physics, politics and more. However, the realm of human knowledge has changed since their day and it is no longer realistically possible for people to attempt to undertake study across the range of the world's problems. There is simply too much information for any one individual to be able to know-ledgeably and credibly criticise such a broad canvas. Instead, scholarship today relies upon painting more detailed imagery on smaller canvases. When one puts all of these canvases together into a gallery we are creating an overview of the world as we know it (the gallery) made up of a number of canvases (subject areas). Politics is simply one canvas in the gallery, along with mathematics, theology, fine art, forestry, pharmacology, mech-anical engineering, classics and many others. While the political canvas shares elements of its subject matter with others (e.g. economics, sociology) and relies upon techniques shared with many (e.g. statistics) it is, at the end of the day, a canvas in its own right, a distinct area of scholarship.

Many have tried to define the nature of the political canvas, but few can agree on a precise definition of its nature. That said, as with a van Gogh, most people can recognise a political issue when they see one. It is not the purpose of this book to enter into this definitional debate, however, worthy as it may be. All readers should be familiar with this debate by the time that they come to write their dissertation and many will have taken entire courses addressing the question 'What is politics?' as part of their degree studies. In Table 1.2 a summary of very basic (and admittedly contested) definitions of the subject matter of the political canvas is given. The remainder of the book will be concerned with the techniques that are used to create and to criticise political pictures.

Given the basic definitions offered in Table 1.2, the author offers the same advice that he offers to first year undergraduates in their first tutorial. That is, regardless of preferred definition, political issues are always going to be issues that are concerned with arguments advanced from within competitive value sys-

*Table 1.2* Some basic definitions of the political canvas

|  | *Definition* |
|---|---|
| Jones *et al.* (1998: 7) | 'Politics is essentially a process which seeks to manage or resolve conflicts of interest between people, usually in a peaceful fashion. In its general sense it can describe the interactions of any group of individuals but in its specific sense it refers to the many and complex relationships which exist between state institutions and the rest of society.' |
| *The Concise Oxford Dictionary*, 7th edn | 'Science and art of government; political affairs or life; political principles'. |
| *The Concise Oxford Dictionary of Politics* | 'A modern mainstream view might be: politics applies only to human beings, or at least to those beings which can communicate symbolically and thus make statements, invoke principles, argue, and disagree. Politics occurs where people disagree about the distribution of reasons and have at least some procedures for the resolution of such disagreements.' |

tems, with the purpose of securing and exercising power (where 'power' is used in its everyday sense as opposed to its more limited Weberian definition). Thus, politics (and its associated sub-fields, e.g. public administration) is an area of scholarly activity that addresses values and power in human society as opposed to natural philosophy which is an area of scholarly activity that addresses the most fundamental questions of the physical world and so on. Taken together, all areas of scholarly activity represent the gallery of human understanding, which, like any gallery, contains old works, new works, the currently fashionable and the currently unfashionable. Your task in completing a dissertation in politics is to develop a thorough understanding of both the subject matter and the techniques associated with the political canvas and to draw conclusions about relevant issues of value and power, employing balance and judgement in the process.

## WHAT IS A DISSERTATION?

A dissertation is an extended piece of personal work. It is far more personal in nature than many other types of academic work. It is an opportunity for you to decide what it is that you will study, how you will study it and, to a certain extent, when you study what. There is no question set, no reading list, no set of lectures to explain the basics of the topic in a structured and summarised fashion and far less opportunity for meaningful discussion with fellow students as to what they think about this matter or that. As we are all different, some students take to this way of working more easily than others do. Some relish the freedom to expand their personal horizons and have an abundance of the self-discipline that is required to undertake their work in a manner that progresses smoothly, finishing their final draft in plenty of time to avoid having to pay a premium rate for last-minute bind-ing. Others of course are less fortunate. Some students can find the dissertation process daunting to say the least. What on earth should I choose to study? Is my problem realistic? How will I approach it? Will I be able to gain access to the necessary resources? Can I do so in the period of time I have remaining, given that I also have a range of other outstanding requirements to complete for my degree and a part-time job? Why is so-and-so not my dissertation tutor? All of these questions can lead to anxiety on the part of the person who asks them, but be warned not to sit and ask them too long. Procrastination, as Shakespeare noted, is the thief of time and the longer you think about prob-lems without taking any steps to address them, the less likely you are to produce your best work. Hopefully the contents of this small volume will help the reader to address some of these questions profitably (although it cannot help with others such as juggling part-time jobs with study or wishing that you had a different dissertation tutor). All that any book can ever do is *assist*; however, remember that this is a personal piece of work and that your personal questions must, in the final analysis, be resolved by you.

The dissertation is also more personal in terms of writing style than many other types of work (although not too personal if the requisite academic tone and balance are to be struck). For instance, if called upon to write a report you would probably set forth in as detached a manner as possible, writing in a fashion not dissimilar to that of a natural scientist. Were you to be called upon to write an essay, while you may bring more of your own ideas to the discussion than you would in a report, the end product will invariably involve weighing up a number of relevant issues through reference to the published ideas of others. In the dissertation you are undertaking a different type of work, even if its subject matter is related to something that you have written about before (e.g. in an essay, a report or some other format).

As noted above, in an essay (or indeed an examination) you will be required to address a given topic, about which you will probably have had at least some lecture material. In writing your essay or examination answer you will almost certainly draw upon materials that were mentioned in lectures and tutorials and that were included on your reading list. This is no bad thing; essentially the essay and the examination are the means by which a member of academic staff assesses your understanding of a fairly substantial chunk of their class. Typically, in addressing the essay or examination question, you will have read around the syllabus with a view to answering questions that are, in comparison with a dissertation, fairly broad. For example, as the author writes this chapter he is looking at the environmental policy paper that he'd set for the Christmas 2000 round of examinations. It includes questions such as, 'With reference to the literature and to environmental events, explain the rise of public environmental concern and green politics over the period 1960–1990' and, 'The "bottom-up approach" can lead to an implementation gap in the policy process. Is this of particular relevance to the successful implementation of environmental policy?'. Whilst (hopefully) reasonable enough as British-style examination questions (although it is always possible that educationalists would throw up their hands in horror), these questions are in fact actually quite general in nature. There is good reason for this of course, as the purpose of the examination is to test knowledge of the environmental policy syllabus. As the basis of a dissertation, however, such questions are unlikely to provide the sort of focus that is required. Essentially, in writing a dissertation you will be addressing a more focused problem than you will probably be used to and doing so in a 'deeper' and more personal way. You truly bring yourself to bear on the final written piece, going way beyond the more limited personal comment that is usually included in the essay or examination answer. You will, in the dissertation, be writing down your own ideas as well as writing about the ideas of others. This can prove one of the most daunting aspects for the dissertation student the first time round. Try to bear in mind that just because ideas have been published in a book or a journal it does not mean that these ideas are de facto better than yours. It just means that they've been aired in public whereas yours haven't. Thus, in writing the dissertation you will be putting your own ideas down on paper to a greater extent than you are used to. Do not worry about this; in writing down his own ideas on how to undertake a dissertation successfully the author has not a clue about how these will be received once published. He has, however, bitten the bullet and agreed to put these ideas down on paper for all who may wish to see them. You will also need to do this (in a balanced, analytical and factually accurate way of course), if you are to produce a high quality dissertation.

As previously noted, also remember that a dissertation is not a textbook. This volume for example would make an appalling dissertation, ranging as it does over such a wide range of issues. The purpose of the dissertation is for you to investigate the area in which you are interested (hopefully being one that you are also easily able to gather the requisite information on) and to demonstrate to the examiner your academic prowess. If you want to write a book, go off and write a book. Don't try to get a book out of a dissertation. Be warned that most PhD students set out with hopes of producing a book from their doctoral thesis (and some do, some don't). Those who do manage to realise their early ambitions often find, however, that the rewriting needed to satisfy a commercial as opposed to a purely academic purpose is so extensive that it would have been easier to have simply written the book from scratch.

Finally, each and every department of politics will expect slightly different things from a dissertation and your tutor should be able to provide you with a checklist of these expectations. Moreover, where departmental advice conflicts with the advice offered in this volume, stick with the former. It is, after all, highly unlikely that it will be the author of this book who will be marking your dissertation.

## DOING A DISSERTATION IN POLITICS

As you read about doing research and writing dissertations you will discover that the field is heavily laden with jargon. For some readers this jargon will be familiar, for others it will not. If you started reading this book on page one then you have already come across the use of terms such as 'ontological'. Perhaps one ought not to be too apologetic about this, however. To some extent it is unavoidable and simply comes with the territory.

Ontology for instance is not really a jargon word at all, it is just not a word that one encounters in everyday conversation. Overall, you will find that a pointed attempt has been made to limit the amount of jargon used in this text. That said, the author's personal experience has suggested that where students take the time to understand ten fundamental concepts (none of which have particularly straightforward names), the processes of planning, undertaking and writing-up a sustained programme of research are made much easier. The ten concepts in question are all covered in the first two chapters of this book and are as follows:

1 Holism
2 Individualism
3 Deduction
4 Induction
5 Qualitative
6 Quantitative
7 Ethical conduct
8 Validity
9 Reliability
10 Representativeness

Thus, having examined the first two of these concepts already, it is now time to turn to concepts 3 and 4, that is, induction and deduction.

## MAKING SENSE OF THE POLITICAL WORLD

Once we have given some thought to what the world is like and identified those parts of the world with which the study of politics is concerned, we then need to consider how political problems are best investigated in order that we may produce a dissertation. This activity is again underpinned by philosophical thought, although now this thought emerges from what are termed 'epistemological' frameworks. There are many epistemological frameworks from which to choose, and it is not the purpose of this book to even list them all, let alone give them full consideration. You are instead directed towards further reading (to be found at the end of this section) should you wish to develop a fuller understanding of epistemological debates.

In the first instance, however, we have to recognise that in the study of politics (as in all social and natural sciences) we deal with two different types of information – theoretical information and empirical information. Theories belong to the kingdom of the mind. They serve as analogues of and explanations for that which surrounds us in the world. Political theories relate therefore to the subjects to be found on the political canvas. Theories are abstractions, created within the human mind and are incredibly useful (there is an old saying that 'there is nothing as practical as a good theory') as they are simplified models of that which surrounds us. If you look at the plates on page xvi you will see three photographs. Plates 1 and 3 represent two competing political theories. You will note that these theoretical interpretations of the political world are, while different, both clear and ordered. You will be able to see from the colour photos shown on the publisher's website that the first theory suggests that the political world is red, orange, yellow, green, blue, indigo, violet, white, grey, black. The second theory suggests that the political world is by contrast blue, white, yellow, black, red, grey, violet, orange, violet and green. (The complementary material on the publisher's website – <http://www.routledge.com/textbooks/doingdissertations.html> – is provided without charge.) Further theories may propose yet further arrangements of the balls of wool, introduce or remove colours altogether or suggest any number of permutations of these possibilities. The potential for generating theories to explain any given problem is therefore more or less limitless. How many theories are there of democracy for example?

The political world that surrounds us is represented by Plate 2. In contrast with theory, the so-called 'empirical' world that is represented by this photograph is messy, unstructured and unordered. This more accurately represents the true nature of the political problems that surround us than Plates 1 and 3. It would, however, be almost impossible to explain this mess as we find it and this is where the theoretical component comes into political research. It allows us to start to make sense of the messy world in which we find ourselves. As Ragin has noted, 'identifying order in the complexity of social life is the most fundamental goal of social research' (Ragin 1994: 30).

Two main epistemological frameworks have driven scientific inquiry down the centuries (although as noted earlier there are many more). These are the inductive and the deductive approaches. The basic difference between these approaches is as shown in Table 1.3.

These epistemological thoughts have a considerable and important part to play in determining the methods used by researchers to address their chosen problem (of which more will be said in Chapter 2). It is sufficient in the meantime to note that regardless of whether a research study is inductive or deductive in character:

> The aim of methods of research is to effect a link between the empirical world, to call it that, and theoretical conceptions of it. By examining the world in a systematic way we can assess the adequacy, plausibility, accuracy, fruitfulness, truth even, of theories about the world.
>
> (Ackroyd and Hughes 1992: 3)

Thus, the vast majority of dissertations in politics will say something about theory (Plates 1 and/or 3) and something about the empirical world (Plate 2). As Martin Bulmer has written:

*Table 1.3* Two basic epistemological stances

| Deductive | Inductive |
| --- | --- |
| Within a deductive study the political researcher takes theory as their starting point. In other words, the research progresses from the adoption of a theoretical position and the prediction of what ought to be found in the empirical world if the theory is a good analogue of that empirical world. The researcher will then proceed to investigate the empirical world in which they find both themselves and their problem in order to test the theory and to draw conclusions about its explanatory value. To refer back to the plates, the researcher essentially starts off at Plate 1 and proceeds to study Plate 2. | Within an inductive study the political researcher takes the empirical world as their starting point. In other words, the research progresses from the investigation of the empirical world in which they find both themselves and their problem. The researcher will then attempt to construct a theoretical explanation of their findings that is consistent with these findings and go on to draw conclusions about whether or not this theory is likely to be of use in making future predictions about the empirical world. To refer back to the plates, the researcher essentially starts off by studying Plate 2 and works towards producing Plate 3. |

Empiricism – the doctrine that factual knowledge has to be clearly established for social understanding – is *not* enough, plausible though the claims of its proponents may be. A mode of social inquiry which produces social facts bereft of theory may be worth while in a number of respects – particularly for policy-making in government – but lacks direction. Conversely, theory alone is empty. The pitfalls of an excessive rationalism – the development of a priori mental constructs into self-contained intellectual systems without any necessary empirical

reference – are that the crucial test of the usefulness and cor-
rectness of a theory which empirical data provide is lacking.

(Bulmer 1984: 38)

However, to take issue with the above quotation and to conclude
this chapter, it is worth noting that while a purely empirical
study will *never* be suitable as a basis for dissertation (i.e. a dissertation cannot be devoid of theory), there are instances where a
purely theoretical study *can* be suitable. In such a study the focus
could for instance involve comparing and contrasting Plates 1
and 3, without regard to the empirical world. This is by no
means an easy option for the dissertation student but is an
option nonetheless. For this reason Chapter 7 will be given over
to discussion of the theoretical dissertation. Finally, if you feel
that you need to read more about the epistemological frameworks underpinning social research (and as previously mentioned, the contents of this chapter are a *very* cursory summary
only) please refer to the following: Ayer (1990); Babbie (1995);
Chalmers (1982); Doyal and Harris (1986); Feyerabend (1975);
Hughes and Sharrock (1997); Keat and Urry (1975); Kuhn
(1970); McNeill (1990); Magee (1982); Papineau (1978);
Russell (1912); Trigg (1985).

## SUMMARY

From this chapter we may conclude:

1  that the dissertation is a *personal* piece of work;
2  that writing a quality dissertation depends on the exercise
   of balance and judgement;
3  that a dissertation is different from the other types of academic work that you've been used to doing;
4  that a dissertation needs to be clearly focused;
5  that a dissertation is not a book;

6  that undertaking a dissertation will undoubtedly involve you having to acquaint yourself with new concepts;

7  that the nature of your dissertation will depend on your view of what the world is like;

8  that the nature of your dissertation will depend on your view of how the world should be studied;

9  that your dissertation will probably address both the theoretical and the empirical (although it may address the theoretical only); and

10  that all of these issues will be further developed as the book progresses.

## TEST YOUR KNOWLEDGE OF THIS CHAPTER

If you want to test your knowledge of this chapter before proceeding to Chapter 2 you can download (free-of-charge from the publisher's website) a set of twenty-five questions to work through at your own pace. You will find answers to the questions provided there also. The website address is again <http://www.routledge.com/textbooks/doingdissertations.html.>
There are also links to the relevant websites at the same address.

This invitation to test your knowledge is repeated at the end of subsequent chapters, where it is only briefly referred to.

# 2

## RESEARCH DESIGN AND THE DISSERTATION

### INTRODUCTION

This chapter stands as the central bridge between the essentially theoretical considerations of Chapter 1 and the entirely practical focus of Chapter 3. As a consequence, the chapter is (perhaps unsurprisingly) half-theoretical and half-practical. As explained in Chapter 1, the key to the sort of academic work that underpins most dissertations is the ability to tie together both theoretical and empirical worlds in a clear and reasoned manner. Moreover, as also noted in Chapter 1, the deductive–inductive dichotomy that permeates academic research, although resulting from philosophical underpinnings, is important in determining what type of study it is that you will undertake for your dissertation. It is from these underpinnings that the qualitative and quantitative traditions of research have taken root, and this chapter will, in the first instance, elucidate further the basic distinctions between these methodological traditions. The remainder of the chapter will be given over to outlining the four key research design principles (validity, reliability, representativeness and ethical conduct) to which due consideration must be given before beginning the detailed planning of a dissertation.

Consequently, this chapter serves to underpin Chapter 3, in which further discussion will be found relating to the practicalities of planning your dissertation. However, before turning to the subject matter in hand, please do bear in mind that the material contained within this chapter by no means represents a detailed account of the qualitative and quantitative research traditions, nor does it represent a detailed account of validity, reliability, representativeness and ethical conduct. Rather, this chapter represents an introduction to these matters, a distillation of the pertinent issues. Further reading is recommended throughout the chapter for those interested in extending their knowledge.

Penultimately then, regarding the relevance of this chapter, it is undoubtedly possible for students to produce high quality dissertations without spending years studying fundamental research design principles. It is however unlikely that a high quality product will result without due consideration being given to the theoretical meaning and practical implications of these principles. Finally, bear in mind that different seats of learning, different dissertation tutors and different examiners have different expectations regarding the extent to which students immerse themselves in the study of these issues. Make sure that you are fully appraised of what is expected of you before you start work on any research proposal. Being so appraised will likely save you time and effort in the long run and remember that as a dissertation student it is *your* responsibility to check the precise nature of your department's and/or tutor's expectations.

## BASIC MODELS OF DISSERTATION RESEARCH

As outlined in Chapter 1, epistemological arguments over the inductive and deductive approaches to problem solving have fed into two main methodological traditions, which are most often classified as the qualitative and the quantitative. Both traditions offer the dissertation student potential means of addressing political problems, in much the same way as they offer potential means of addressing problems to those working in other fields e.g. economics, management, psychology and sociology as well as in the natural scientific and technological spheres. The epistemological arguments of induction versus deduction underpinning these traditions have of course raged for centuries and, as with most philosophical arguments, are no closer to resolution at the turn of the twenty-first century than they were at the turn of the twentieth. Of course the purpose of this book is not to get bogged down in extended discussion of these issues, but to examine their relevance to the student who needs to produce as good a dissertation as possible within strict time and resource constraints.

Bearing this entirely practical objective in mind, it is sufficient to state here that inductive reasoning has made a greater contribution to the development of the qualitative tradition of social scientific research than it has to the quantitative. Conversely, it can also be stated that deductive reasoning has contributed more to the development of the quantitative tradition of social scientific research than it has to the qualitative. This is not to make any general claim about the relationships between induction, deduction, qualification and quantification however. Rather, it is more appropriate to state that while there are undoubtedly relationships between inductive reasoning and qualitative methods and between deductive reasoning and quantitative methods, it is by no means impossible for a dissertation student to undertake a study that employs for example both inductive reasoning and quantification. Thus, before turning to consider the qualitative and quantitative traditions of social scientific research further, it is important to conclude that while the two traditions are respectively associated with inductive and deductive reasoning, this is best regarded as just this, i.e. a relationship of association rather than one of necessity.

## Basic model of dissertation research 1: qualitative

In the first instance, it must be noted that the qualitative tradition has a particularly important role to play in political research. It is a methodological tradition that encourages the researcher to make sense of their chosen political problem through personal academic interpretation. It is an unashamedly subjective tradition and is none the poorer for that. Do not make the common error of assuming a subjective approach to be somehow invalid in political research; it is only so if clearly unbalanced. Indeed, it is the interpretive backbone of the qualitative tradition that makes it of central importance to political research. Look back at Chapter 1 and consider the definition of politics provided therein. If it is accepted that political questions are in large part questions about values then it seems not unreasonable to suggest that they be addressed in a manner that will fully allow for reasoned consideration of these values.

In terms of definitions, then, the qualitative tradition of social research is generally regarded as involving the focused study of a small-scale problem using interpretive (as opposed to say statistical) techniques. Such an approach is usually adopted with a view to developing a 'deep' rather than a 'broad' understanding of the chosen problem and drawing conclusions that relate directly to this problem thereafter. Consider these words of Roy Preece, 'To qualify is to ascribe a quality, or to describe a thing. The study of literature, for example, could be seen as largely qualitative' (Preece 1994: 41). He adds the following:

> Qualitative methods, however, should not be seen as mere description. Though numerical procedures are not essentially involved, logical testing and argument are just as important in, for example, history and law, or the qualitative parts of geography, as in more quantitative disciplines.
>
> (Preece 1994: 42)

For further definitions of the qualitative tradition of social scientific research please see Babbie (1995: glossary), Blaxter *et al.* (1996: 60), Creswell (1994: 1), Gilbert (1993: 7), Hakim (2000: 34) and Strauss and Corbin (1990: 19).

As previously noted, this book is not the place to provide detailed accounts of the epistemological roots of the qualitative approach. However, of particular relevance to the modern development of this approach are the notions of 'hermeneutics' and 'verstehen'. These terms are unfortunately indicative of the jargon-laden nature of the subject matter, but can be simplified as meaning 'interpretation' and 'empathy' respectively. In other words, undertaking a qualitative dissertation will rely on the student's ability to interpret and/or empathise. As so much political research is based upon the interpretive approach it is sensible (just to show that if and when you come across the term elsewhere it isn't something to be baffled by) to define hermeneutics here as being, 'the theory and practice of interpretation. We are no longer proclaiming our "disengagement" from our subject matter as a condition of science (positivism), but our "commitment" and "engagement" as a condition of understanding social life' (May 1997: 14).

As far as verstehen is concerned, this is likely to be less relevant to students of politics than it is to students of some of the other social sciences. Do, however, be aware that the epistemological heritage of verstehen is clearly outlined in the works of Max Weber. Thus, should you wish to find out more about empathetic investigation, refer to any textbook on Weber, for instance Giddens (1971), Parkin (1982).

## Basic model of dissertation research 2: quantitative

At the outset, it must be noted that the quantitative tradition also has an important role to play in political research. Quantitative methods are, admittedly, less likely to be used by dissertation students in the United Kingdom than their qualitative cousins are, but this may well be a result of the largely interpretive manner in which politics are taught in the British educational system. However, (and this comment is based on a qualitative analysis of purely personal observation as opposed to any determined fact), the author is going to risk his neck here and suggest that colleagues elsewhere often at least appear more at ease with the quantitative approach. Consequently, you may find that you are reading this book in a country, an institution or a department in which the quantitative approach is the normal mode of dissertation research. The most important point here, however, is that regardless of whether you are to undertake a quantitative or a qualitative study, make sure that you have access to at least one member of staff who has experience of doing that type of research. This person need not be your main dissertation tutor, but the suggestion here is that it would be sheer folly to embark upon a dissertation without having at least established that there is scope for meaningful critical feedback on your method.

The quantitative approach is of course the norm in the study of natural sciences and technology and is also widely used in the social subjects (especially some branches of economics and psychology). It is a methodological tradition that encourages the dissertation student to make sense of their chosen political problem through the use of numbers, which are employed as either measures or indicators of relevant variables (there will be further explanation of this point in Chapter 5). The analysis of these numbers tends to rely upon the application of techniques that are statistical as opposed to mathematical. If you bear in mind that most basic statistical functions are essentially 'clever arithmetic', this means that most students are able to undertake quantitative research. There is no need for advanced trigonometry or calculus (unless that is you personally feel an urge to adopt such techniques).

Moreover, in much the same way as a warning was earlier issued about misplaced assumptions regarding subjectivity and its role in the study of politics, be wary of assuming that the inclusion of numerical data necessarily implies objectivity. It is now nearly fifty years since the publication of *How to Lie with Statistics* (Huff 1954). Anyone who is tempted to confuse quantification with objectivity is politely directed towards this small gem.

In terms of definitions though, the quantitative tradition of social research is generally regarded as involving the representative study of a well-defined problem using statistical techniques. Such an approach is often adopted with a view to developing a reliable understanding of the chosen problem and drawing conclusions that can be applied beyond the problem itself. Consider again the words of Roy Preece: 'To quantify is used in the sense of to ascribe a quantity to a thing, and the process is known as quantification' (1994: 41). He continues, 'Quantitative methods generally have developed further to include not merely counting and measuring but also the powerful analytical procedures of statistics and many other techniques such as mathematical modelling and linear programming' (ibid.: 42).

For further definitions of the quantitative tradition of social scientific research see Ackroyd and Hughes (1992: 42), Allan and Skinner (1991: 215), Babbie (1995: glossary), Creswell (1994: 117), Gilbert (1993: 7) and Ragin (1994: 131).

As with considerations of the qualitative tradition, this book is not the place to provide detailed accounts of the epistemological roots of the quantitative approach (there are several). However, of particular relevance to its modern application are notions of 'positivism' and developments thereof. This term can be defined thus:

> We can characterize this tradition in the same terms as the aims of natural science: the prediction and explanation of the behaviour of phenomena and the pursuit of objectivity, which is defined as the researcher's 'detachment' from the topic under investigation ... positivism explains human behaviour in terms of cause and effect ...
>
> (May 1997: 10)

Note from the above that it is the researcher's detachment that is identified as being the determinant of objectivity, rather than the numerical nature of the data gathered. Finally, to conclude this section, it ought to be explained that positivism and other epistemological developments thereof advocate the adoption of a deductive approach in research (although there are also inductive models of quantitative social scientific inquiry). Should you wish to find out more about the various branches of epistemological thought that have shaped quantitative investigation, you are advised to refer to the following basic sources as opposed to elementary textbooks (because they are often clearer): Ayer (1990), Durkheim (1964), Kuhn (1970), Popper (1969) and Russell (1912).

## QUALITATIVE AND QUANTITATIVE COMPARISON

There are, then, two main traditions of research with which this book will concern itself: the qualitative and the quantitative. Choice of appropriate method is central to the production of a successful dissertation but is an activity that is subsequent to problem definition. It is with this in mind the following statement was framed: *never choose your method first*. Do not for example decide at the outset that you either do or do not wish to undertake quantitative work. Rather, choose your topic first and then fit the appropriate method to the problem. How you can do this in preparing a research proposal will form the basis of Chapter 3.

As seen in Chapters 1 and 2, though, both qualitative and quantitative methods have a role to play in political research. Furthermore, as previously noted in this chapter, 'Both traditions offer the dissertation student potential means of addressing political problems,' and this needs to be remembered throughout the early stages of dissertation planning (i.e. the methods ought only to be chosen once a clear problem has been identified). This idea of placing the early focus on problem definition is supported by Ackroyd and Hughes who note:

> It is the nature of the research problem that should dictate the appropriate research method; sometimes quantification is required, sometimes not. There is no intrinsic virtue to either style of method. What we are being asked to choose between are promissory notes, not achievements. There is a great deal wrong with quantitative methods just as there is a great deal wrong with qualitative ones. Both kinds are, as it were, in much the same boat.
>
> (Ackroyd and Hughes 1992: 30)

Moreover, should you be in any doubt as to the veracity of Ackroyd and Hughes' statement, consider the following quotations as well, the first of which relates to the qualitative approach, the second to the quantitative:

> Qualitative research can be accused of being unscientific, unrepresentative, open to bias and, even, to manipulation, conscious or unconscious.
>
> (Preece 1994: 43)

> Consider the researcher who wants to understand the fascin-
> ation that some people have with guns – for example, gun
> collectors, some military personnel, hunters, and other
> enthusiasts. A big-picture view might show that certain cat-
> egories of people (for example, lower middle-class white
> males) are more likely to collect guns and subscribe to maga-
> zines devoted to guns … But does the big-picture view really
> say very much about the fascination with guns?
>
> (Ragin 1994: 81)

In other words, prior to undertaking dissertation research one ought to be aware that both qualitative and quantitative approaches have a place within the family of political research techniques but that neither is by any means a panacea. Please do not be led by a pre-existing preference for one method over another in choosing a dissertation study (although many prob-lems can be addressed in a number of different ways).

You ought to be led to an appropriate method by consider-ation of your problem. If you are unsure as to which method is most appropriate for your problem, ask your dissertation tutor for advice when the time comes (i.e. once you have a clearly defined problem in hand). Finally, for further information on the quantitative and qualitative comparison you could do far worse than consulting John Creswell's volume *Research Design: Qualitative and Quantitative Approaches* (Creswell: 1994).

## QUALITATIVE AND QUANTITATIVE COMPATIBILITY?

Let us return to the statement 'Both traditions offer the disserta-tion student potential means of addressing political problems,' again. Might it be possible that both quantitative and qualitative methods can be usefully employed side by side in the same study? We already know there are a wide range of epi-stemological stances underpinning the various methods used in political research, many of which are essentially incompatible. From a philosophical point of view, then, it is a sin to combine method A with method B if these have been built upon fundamentally distinctive foundations. However, in the cold light of day, most politics students will not be undertaking philosophical dissertations (and where they choose to do so are more likely to focus on a key element of political philosophy such as social justice rather than on epistemology). In purely pragmatic terms, the consequence of this is that if one accepts the fundamental tensions that may be present between opposing epistemological stances, one can then go on to mix and match methods within the same study, sometimes to good effect. The philosophical tensions will always be there in the work, but only on a philosophical level; in other words, for a great many dissertations the existence of such philosophical tensions matters not one jot. Do check with your dissertation tutor if you end up planning to mix and match methods, however. Although most departments are now happy for students to undertake such research not all are. If you are studying in a department where mixing and matching is not encouraged, do bear in mind that there are real theoretical concerns about the employment of such an approach, even if it can yield practical benefits.

Where qualitative and quantitative methods are both used within the same study this is termed 'triangulation'. Note from the quotation below the not inconsiderable pragmatic benefits that can be derived from the adoption of this approach (but do not lose sight of the dogmatic problems that can be associated with philosophical inconsistency):

> Triangulating ... refers to the attempt to strengthen the validity of empirical evidence in social science by reliance on more than one approach. When a hypothesis can survive the confrontation of a series of complementary methods of testing,

> it contains a degree of validity unattainable by a hypothesis
> tested with the more constricted framework of a single method.
> (Bulmer 1984: 32)

Thus, to conclude this section, bear in mind that both qualitative and quantitative methods bring strengths and weaknesses to political research and that (on a pragmatic level anyway) these different methods can be usefully combined to create a stronger piece of research as a basis for a dissertation. There are however philosophical inconsistencies associated with this approach. You do need to be aware of this. However, in knowing about and acknowledging these inconsistencies you will not (in this author's view at least) detract from the standard of a dissertation by mixing and matching methods to suit the problem. To repeat, do check with your dissertation tutor before adopting any method. You will find that some departments may be less keen on triangulation than others. Where the latter is the case there are good reasons for it.

Nevertheless, triangulation is widely accepted nowadays as being a valid approach to adopt in dissertation research. The main reason for this is that the qualitative and quantitative methods add different strengths to a study as far as maximising attainment of the fundamental research principles of validity, reliability and representativeness are concerned.

## KEY RESEARCH DESIGN PRINCIPLES

It is no accident that McNeill (1990) and Hughes and Sharrock (1997) are in complete agreement (as indeed are more or less all authors) that all methods of social inquiry ought to be as valid as possible, as reliable as possible and as representative as possible. In the most simplistic analysis of why this is important, an examiner who deems a dissertation to be valid, reliable and representative, is more likely to award a high mark to that dissertation.

See the bullet paragraphs below for a brief synopsis of these principles:

- in a *valid* dissertation the evidence gathered will be an accurate reflection of the evidence sought (i.e. is entirely relevant to the problem). This is primarily achieved through the logical process of 'unpacking' or 'operationalising' the problem (of which more in Chapter 3);
- in a *reliable* study the methods of inquiry used ought to produce the same (or at least very similar) results every time, irrespective of who carries out the inquiry or of where and when it is carried out (assuming that is, replication of method);
- in a *representative* piece of research the variables studied can be considered by and large to be typical. For example, in a study of voting behaviour, what was the percentage of working class subjects included in the sample and was this typical? In a study of manifesto contents have all the main parties' manifestos been identified and consulted?

As previously stated, different methods have different strengths and weaknesses and it is not always possible to maximise the attainment of all three principles within the confines of a one-off dissertation study. The student will often have to horse-trade with themselves (and with their tutor) regarding the extent to which such principles are upheld within the practicalities of realising their dissertation. In other words, it must be stated here that while it is often asserted that the attainment of all three principles is a *necessity* for any successful study, such an approach is in fact a theoretical, ideal-type model of dissertation research. It is rare to encounter a study (and in this the author includes studies much larger than those required to produce a sound dissertation) that clearly measures up to the stringent requirements of this ideal-type model. As with triangulation, we see here an example of the distinction between theoretical and empirical worlds. That is, while in theory one should always aim to uphold the ideal-type, practicalities often demand otherwise. Again, in a manner similar to considering whether there are practical advantages to be derived from triangulation, in planning your dissertation you need to be aware of the practical constraints faced when doing research in the real world. If you are unable to maximise validity, reliability and representativeness all at the same time you will need to horse-trade. If this is the case, seek your dissertation tutor's advice on which of the key principles you could compromise on within the ambit of your dissertation aims. Compromise is not something that anyone wishes to make within a piece of academic work, but it is an unfortunate fact of life that it is often necessary.

The last but by no means the least of the key research design principles is that of ethical conduct. This principle has been separated from the other three for good reason. Namely, in this author's view at least, because it should not be included in any horse-trading equation. In other words, what is being suggested here is that while, as with the other three principles, one *can* choose to forgo ethical conduct in favour of maximising attainment of one of the other key principles, *this should not be done*. Although you may read elsewhere of the merits of acting unethically in order to increase validity for example, you are strongly advised here against pursuing such a course. If others are happy to compromise regarding ethical conduct then let them do so. I urge *you* not to compromise this principle, especially in dissertation research. How would you feel if your valid, reliable and representative research were to result in a poor dissertation mark as a result of ethical concerns on the part of the examiners? Should you find yourself facing a serious dilemma that may involve compromising ethical conduct, think again about your topic. It is better to change the topic altogether than to proceed without due regard to high ethical standards.

## Key research design principle 1: ethical conduct

Research ethics are usually a subset of a broader set of professional ethics. For example, medical research ethics are a subset of medical ethics and political research ethics are part and parcel of the broader professional framework within which political researchers should work. To see a relevant example please refer to *A Guide to Ethics in Political Science* (American Political Science Association Committee on Professional Ethics, Rights and Freedoms: 1991). Ethical requirements are not dissimilar for qualitative and quantitative studies, i.e. both traditions of research place great value on ethical conduct.

A rare benefit enjoyed by those working in the social sciences when compared to researchers in other fields (in biology and medicine especially) is that the ethical issues encountered are less likely to produce the sort of heated debate associated with procedures such as vivisection, genetic modification or the production of clones. This does not of course mean that there cannot be serious ethical concerns associated with social scientific research – it's just that these concerns are less likely to provoke the sort of deeply emotive responses associated with research in other areas. Moreover, take heed of the words of Earl Babbie below. Do be aware of ethical subtleties and try to think marginally (because, as ever, there is a thin dividing line between what is marginally acceptable and what is marginally unacceptable):

> Any of us can immediately see that a study that requires the torturing of small children is unethical. I know you'd speak out immediately if I suggested we interview people about their sex lives and then publish what they said in the local newspaper. But, as ethical as you are, you'd totally miss the ethical issue in some other situations – not because you're bad, but because we all do that.
>
> (Babbie 1995: 447)

However, you can take heart from the fact that in much the same way as social researchers are less likely to encounter serious ethical problems than say bio-medical researchers, the political researcher is indeed less likely to face ethical problems than social scientists working in some other fields (e.g. psychology). Babbie (1995) summarises the work of many commentators when he outlines five main areas that can give rise to ethical concern in social scientific research. These five areas have been listed and elaborated upon below. You will see that all that is asked of you is basic common decency.

- *Voluntary participation*    People should not be press-ganged into assisting you with your research. Bear in mind that people (including university staff) are also free to withdraw any offer of assistance at any subsequent point, no matter how difficult this may be for you to swallow at the time. The author had personal experience of such a withdrawal of assistance after a full year of doctoral research (as a result of a personnel change within an organisation). No matter how frustrating it is if people refuse or withdraw assistance, remember that they are free to do so at their own pleasure and there is nothing that you can do about it. Hopefully not too many readers will have to cope with this unfortunate fact of life. In trying to encourage assistance from others the following do not go amiss (even if contrary to your normal mode of operation): be polite; be suitably deferential without toadying; be smart in your appearance; and, take great care with the clarity of your communication, written, verbal and non-verbal alike.
- *No harm to the participants*    Here, 'harm' primarily means causing unease. Doing a dissertation in politics is unlikely to cause anyone physical harm, but do take account of people's sensitivities. For example, never be openly dismissive of people's political views as these are, after all, probably as

dear to them as yours are to you. Moreover, avoid asking people how much they get paid, this is a sure-fire way to annoy them.

- *Anonymity and confidentiality*  These are two different (yet oft-confused) concepts. The basic difference is that where someone helps anonymously you do not know who it was that gave you certain assistance. Where someone helps you confidentially you do know who gave you what assistance but do not acknowledge this fact (other than by a letter of thanks to the individual concerned for example). Even if the people who have helped have identified themselves to you, unless they clearly indicate otherwise you would be safest to treat any assistance received as confidential. Other issues connected to confidentiality can include issues regarding the legal and ethical position on ownership of data (e.g. if you have been given a copy of a document for information only, do not then start quoting from it – writing a dissertation is not a journalistic pursuit and you're unlikely to be able to defend such an action). Finally, make sure that you are aware of relevant data protection law, especially if you are likely to hold any data relating to individuals that were not drawn from a publicly available source. Within an educational establishment you will normally find the library staff to be well appraised of current data protection law. If in doubt, seek advice.
- *Deceiving subjects*  This would generally be through the adoption of covert methods of research. You will often read elsewhere of covert studies being undertaken with a view to enhancing the validity of data gathered. Indeed, the author has himself been engaged in this type of research in the past. It is not however something that he is at all proud of, nor is it something that he would wish to repeat. No matter how much one justifies such actions to oneself, the fact remains that even small-scale deception and 'white lies' are, at the end of the day, deception and lies.

- *Faithful analysis and reporting*   You must avoid all the academic sins of which you should be fully aware by now when it comes to writing a dissertation. These sins include purposeful misrepresentation of the position of others, inaccurate reproduction of quotations, inventing data (whether quotations or numerical data), adding titles to the bibliography that you have not read, slack referencing and – chief amongst the academic sins – plagiarism. Should you be tempted to indulge in any of these practices it is hereby suggested that you check your institution's academic regulations first. Although penalties for such activities vary from institution to institution they are uniformly harsh. The author has himself sat on an examination board that has stripped an award from a student for plagiarism in a dissertation and has heard of similar cases from colleagues. Do not take the risk.

To conclude this section of the chapter on a more positive note, however, it is sufficient simply to repeat the earlier warning: do not compromise ethical standards for methodological advantage. Better to choose a new dissertation topic than to proceed unethically. Finally, should any readers be interested in further developing their knowledge in this field you are directed towards Babbie (1995), Homan (1991), Kimmel (1988), May (1997), Punch (1986) Sieber (1992).

## Key research design principle 2: validity

As previously noted in this chapter, 'in a *valid* dissertation the evidence gathered will be an accurate reflection of the evidence sought (i.e. is entirely relevant to the problem)'. Thus, the pursuit of validity in dissertation research is, in everyday language, best described as the pursuit of accuracy. Accuracy is of course a fundamental cornerstone of all academic work. Think for example about the differences that exist between scholarship and journalism. For instance, 1,500 words can be enough for a journalist to conclude that Parliament has undoubtedly gone to the dogs. By contrast, an academic could easily spend a lifetime studying Parliament before coming to the conclusion that it may or may not be going to the dogs. Of course, it is undoubtedly the case that the journalist's conclusions will be more accessible, more entertaining and more likely to put some fire in your belly. The academic's conclusions will, however, for all that their character is comparatively staid and cautious, probably be more accurate (indeed, note the use of the word 'probably' here to increase the accuracy of the sentence). This is not a criticism of journalism, just an example of different styles of working to meet different sets of fundamental aims.

In undertaking a dissertation in politics, it is essential that your work is as accurate as possible. Admittedly, we are a long way off from bringing the same sort of precision to solving political problems as a physicist is able to bring to their investigations into the problems of natural philosophy. Indeed (whilst not wishing to get involved in soothsaying) it is entirely possible that methods leading to such levels of accuracy will *never* be available to the political researcher. That is not to say that the validity of any proposed piece of dissertation research should not be given close and careful consideration, however.

Although you will find reference to a range of different types of validity elsewhere (e.g. Babbie (1995) mentions four – 'face validity', 'criterion-related validity', 'construct validity' and 'content validity') it is the two latter categories that have special significance for the student of politics as far as ensuring accuracy is concerned. Both content and construct validity are primarily ensured by clear thinking, although content validity is the simpler of the two to ensure.

If the author of a dissertation can adequately demonstrate to the examiner that the variables selected for study adequately match that study's conceptual aims then it will be said that the dissertation has *content validity*. For instance, Babbie writes: 'If we say we are measuring prejudice *in general*, do our measurements reflect prejudice against racial and ethnic groups, religious minorities, women, the elderly, and so on?' (1995: 128). Alternatively, consider a dissertation investigating the role of political participation by citizens in modern liberal democracies. A comparative study of the United Kingdom and France *would* have content validity whereas a comparative study of the United Kingdom and the People's Republic of China *would not*.

As noted above, ensuring *construct validity* is also of central importance to the coherence of any dissertation in politics (although ensuring construct as opposed to content validity can prove to be more taxing for students). Building construct validity into a dissertation does, however, rely upon the same basic skill, i.e. clarity of thought. Further attention will be paid to this issue in Chapter 3.

In the meantime remember that social scientific research is usually about the interplay of theory and the empirical world. Given that so much political research sets out to examine the relationships between the theoretical and empirical worlds, there is a need to clearly link the two worlds together through research aims or hypotheses. It is this 'linking' process that provides construct validity. If the process by which we translate abstract concepts into a list of 'real' things for investigation is done in a logical fashion (the cumbersome term *operationalisation* is often used to describe this process) we will have demonstrated construct validity. This process may sound much more complex than it actually is and, as already noted, a fuller explanation of how to work through it is to be found in Chapter 3.

To sum up this section then, it is worth stating here that although the relationship is (as ever) one of association rather than one of necessity, the extent to which qualitative methods can ensure validity is often held up as being their most meritorious facet. Conversely, the quantitative approach is sometimes criticised as lacking validity (a criticism which is sometimes, but by no means always, a reasonable one). For an example of this critical argument refer back to the quotation from Ragin (1994) reproduced earlier in this chapter (the one relating to people's fascination with firearms, p. 29). Finally, the validity of quantitative and qualitative methods will be further investigated in Chapters 5 and 6 respectively. Should readers wish to seek further information on the various types of validity (including those not covered here, i.e. face- and criterion-related) please refer to one or more of the following texts: Babbie (1995); Bouma and Atkinson (1995); Hughes and Sharrock (1997); McNeill (1990); de Vaus (1996).

### Key research design principle 3: reliability

At the outset it must be noted that of all the key research principles, 'reliability' is the one which tends to cause the greatest degree of confusion for students. The reason for this is straightforward enough. In everyday life we often use the word 'reliable' to refer to something that we consider accurate. For instance, if we regard a source of gossip as being 'reliable', in so doing we are assuming that this source is an accurate and credible one. In the world of academic research however, the word 'reliability' is best translated as meaning 'consistency'. Thus, a conflict is evident between the way in which the word is used as we go about our everyday business and the way in which it is used in the more limited academic sense. As Babbie has noted, 'In the abstract, reliability is a matter of whether a particular technique, applied repeatedly to the same object, would yield the same result each time' (1995: 124).

In general terms then, a study is regarded as reliable if its results can be reproduced regardless of who it was carried out by and where or when they did this. In all honesty, the term has been adopted wholesale from the natural sciences and as a consequence there are a range of problems associated with its use in connection with social research. Consider the nature of much natural scientific investigation – observing the effects of gravity for example. It matters not whether you are Galileo Galilei apocryphally standing at the top of the leaning tower of Pisa in the sixteenth century, Isaac Newton sitting under an English apple tree in the seventeenth century or somebody who dropped a wallet full of Dollars in New Zealand five minutes ago. Such a scientific investigation is an investigation into a problem that has a universal nature (in the true sense of 'universal'). In other words the 'who', 'where' and 'when' factors in the investigations are more or less rendered redundant by the very nature of the problem. Consequently, if 'who', 'where' or 'when' were to have any bearing on the results of such natural scientific research into a universal problem, then it would seriously threaten the validity of that research also (as these factors would have exerted undue influence on the accuracy as well as on the consistency of the results).

The basic nature of most social scientific problems is different. The problems faced by political researchers and by other social scientists are, more often than not, far from universal. Indeed most of the problems that the political researcher will investigate are very much problems of 'here and now' (or, alternatively, of 'there and then'). In other words, political problems are usually culturally and temporally bound (and this can be as true of theoretical problems as of empirical ones). One consequence of this is that the 'where' and 'when' factors play a large part both in the framing of a problem and in its solution. For instance, consider a study into the extent to which a Monarch is able to influence the legislative process. Regardless of the adoption of identical methods, very different conclusions would be reached were the study to have been conducted in Russia in 1900 and in adjoining Norway in 2000. What we have here is an example of a problem that is far from universal. It is an example of a problem that is bound by both cultural and temporal factors. Indeed, it is a problem that only really makes sense within these boundaries. Consequently, given the central relevance of 'where' and 'when' to the very nature of so many of our political problems, it is not entirely unreasonable to argue that (in the strict sense at least) the notion of reliability can, in this field of study, actually be regarded as a bit of a white elephant.

Putting theoretical considerations to one side there is still a clear need to control the 'who' factor in social research to the best of our abilities. For example, although the qualitative tradition is based upon subjective interpretation (and as such is generally regarded as being less reliable than the quantitative tradition – see Chapters 5 and 6 for further relevant discussion) such subjective analysis must *at least appear credible* to an examiner (whether or not they necessarily agree with it). In other words, ensuring reliability in political research is primarily about eliminating undue bias at the various points at which it can creep into a study. Examples of how to do this are shown next.

1   During the dissertation's planning stage make sure that you become acquainted with the contents of this and other volumes on dissertation research in the social sciences. You will also need to develop a thorough understanding of the various data gathering and analytical tools that are available to you. Such an understanding may of course be developed through attendance at classes in research methods where these are available. If your department does not offer such formal classes then you are strongly advised to spend a good deal of time developing the requisite knowledge yourself (through consulting the suggestions for further reading that are peppered throughout this volume).

2   When the time comes to gather your data there are three

main ways in which you can enhance reliability. First, try to adopt methods that others have successfully employed previously. There is rarely merit in inventing methods of your own and little point in re-inventing the wheel. Bear in mind that the more faithfully you follow a pre-established method (assuming of course that it is not one which has been discredited) the more reliable your research will be. Second (and especially if using a quantitative model), *use established measures to classify your variables* in conjunction with an established method. For instance, if you are in the United Kingdom, use the Government's standardised Socio-Economic Groups (SEGs) as a means of classifying economic status and social class. Third (and of particular relevance to quantitative studies involving questionnaires and the like), be aware that a great many publications exist such as, *Standardised Questions for Tourism Surveys* (Scottish Tourist Board Planning and Development Division: 1993). By using pre-tested question formats you not only improve the reliability of your research but also save yourself a good deal of time and effort. Worthy of special mention here is *The Question Bank*, accessible via the website of the University of Surrey (http://qb.soc.surrey.ac.uk/). This is a very valuable resource, containing a wealth of pre-tested questions relevant to the student of politics and well worth a visit.

3  At the analytical stage of your research ensure that if doing quantitative work you follow established procedure. If on the other hand you are undertaking a qualitative study the analysis of data can prove to be fairly problematic in so far as demonstrating reliability is concerned. As noted previously this process of analysis is subjective by definition, yet needs to at least appear credible to an examiner. In all honesty, the best way in which to improve the reliability of qualitative analysis is to ask your tutor for detailed commentary at the draft dissertation stage.

4 You may well come across other means of enhancing reliability in the literature. Examples of such methods include the testing of *research worker reliability* and the use of techniques such as the *test-retest* and *split-half* methods (Babbie 1995: 125–7). These are however unlikely to be of direct relevance to a student undertaking a dissertation in politics. If interested in reading more about reliability in the social sciences, please refer to Babbie (1995), Bouma and Atkinson (1995), McNeill (1990), de Vaus (1996).

## Key research design principle 4: representativeness

The fourth and final key principle of research design is representativeness. It is essentially a statistical concept and, further to the brief description offered earlier in this chapter, can be defined thus:

> That quality of a sample of having the same distribution of characteristics as the population from which it was selected. By implication, descriptions and explanations derived from an analysis of the sample may be assumed to *represent* similar ones in the population.
>
> (Babbie 1995: glossary)

Representativeness is a simpler concept to understand than either validity or reliability and is of special importance when undertaking quantitative research. Indeed, questions will be asked if the sampling strategy used to underpin a piece of dissertation research is not both apparent and appropriate. On the other hand, within the qualitative model (where the research focus is upon the examination of a smaller number of cases in greater depth), one has to accept that studies undertaken using such methods are regularly (even normally) unrepresentative. Proponents of the qualitative tradition ardently contend that what is gained in terms of accuracy (from the depth of investigation) more than offsets the lack of ability to generalise from the particular cases studied. As far as this horse-trading between validity and representativeness is concerned the supporters of the qualitative tradition can also take heart from the fact that if political problems are so often culturally and temporally bound, there is a less pressing need to be able to generalise from research findings.

To return to representativeness, however, it most certainly is not the author's intention to go into detailed explanations here of how to draw samples, how to work out sampling fractions or of how to interpret response rates. Some of this material will be addressed in Chapter 5, but in truth *any* basic book on statistics will provide the reader with the information that they are likely to need should they end up doing a representative quantitative dissertation. In very simplistic terms, the stages involved in drawing a sample are as follows:

1  Identify the population that you wish to study. In the statistical sense the term 'population' is used to define the total number of known instances (where an instance can basically be anything that you wish e.g. in some studies it may be a person, in others a statutory instrument and in others a Ministerial portfolio).

2  Generally speaking whole populations tend to be too large to study. Where the chosen population is too large, we must then proceed to draw a sample of it for closer examination. (Note that the greater the proportion of the population sampled the more representative your study will be, although this is a geometrical as opposed to an arithmetical relationship.)

A variety of means by which representative samples can be drawn exist, some of which are better suited to certain types of problem than others. The means of drawing representative samples include random, periodic, stratified, cluster and quota sampling. You will find that further information on these techniques can be gleaned from any basic book on statistics, but do be warned to be particularly wary of the merits of quota sampling. Moreover, from time to time there are also good reasons for focusing a study upon a non-representative sample, i.e. purposely electing to place a clear emphasis on a given section of the population. Drawing such a sample (by a process known as *weighted sampling*) will give us a disproportionate sample and thereby focus the study on a particular segment of the population. This approach is by no means uncommon: for instance, if you wished to evaluate the effectiveness of a governmental grant scheme in terms of meeting policy goals, it is not unreasonable to wish to focus your attentions on those persons or organisations that have been in receipt of a grant.

There are still further types of sampling, which are neither representative nor weighted – for instance 'snowball' sampling. As suggested earlier however, this is not the place to hold an extended discussion of the detailed ins and outs of sampling procedure. Although the concept of representativeness as it relates to data analysis will be referred to again in Chapters 5 and 8, most of the relevant issues pertaining to the pursuit of representativeness are more appropriately (and also better) explained in basic statistical textbooks than here. Consequently, you are directed towards the statistical shelfmarks of your library for further information, although you may find the following basic sources of particular assistance: Babbie (1995); Black (1993); McNeill (1990); Saunders *et al.* (1997).

## SUMMARY

From this chapter we may conclude:

1 that there are two traditions of social scientific research that are of relevance to the dissertation student – the qualitative and the quantitative;

2 that the qualitative tradition is very commonly used to address political problems in dissertations as it is in large part reliant upon the subjective interpretation of non-numerical information;

3 that the quantitative tradition, nowadays associated in the main with the deductivist camp and utilising statistical analysis to draw conclusions, is also pertinent to the solution of many political problems;

4 that the qualitative and quantitative traditions each offer a range of advantages to the student undertaking a dissertation in politics but that each has drawbacks also;

5 that the qualitative and quantitative traditions are not, in a pragmatic sense at least, mutually exclusive and can be usefully combined in dissertation research;

6 that all dissertation research should be undertaken in an ethical fashion;

7 that, as far as is practically possible, dissertation research should be valid (i.e. accurate) and that qualitative methods are regarded as being especially valid;

8 that, as far as is practically possible, dissertation research should be reliable (i.e. consistent) and while quantitative methods are more reliable than qualitative, reliability cannot be attained in anything like the same way as in natural science;

9 that, as far as is practically possible, dissertation research should be representative, although qualitative dissertations in particular are often unrepresentative; and

10  that it is rarely possible to maximise attainment of all four key research design principles (i.e. ethical conduct, validity, reliability and representativeness) in one study. Thus, students regularly have to trade the attainment of one or more of the key principles off against one or more of the others (with the proviso that ethical conduct alone should not be compromised). See Table 2.1 for examples of such trade-offs.

*Table 2.1* Examples of trade-offs between the four key research design principles

|  | *Validity* | *Reliability* | *Representativeness* |
|---|---|---|---|
| *Ethical conduct* | Deceiving subjects often leads to improved levels of validity as regards findings, but is clearly unethical | Ensuring anonymity of research participants is ethical, but weakens reliability (as the study is difficult to repeat) | Ignoring principle of voluntary participation may improve representativeness but is unethical |
| *Validity* | | Undertaking qualitative work maximises validity at the expense of reliability | Undertaking quantitative work can threaten validity but maximises representativeness |
| *Reliability* | | | Reliable repetition of a previous study may not account for cultural change over time and can result in drawing a sample that is no longer representative |

A thorough understanding of all this material is crucial in underpinning the next chapter, which aims, through building upon these key principles, to suggest in greater detail how to begin the dissertation process in earnest, i.e. addressing the development of a thorough plan of action in the shape of a research proposal.

## TEST YOUR KNOWLEDGE OF THIS CHAPTER

Please refer to p. 19 for details.

# 3

## DEFINING THE PROBLEM

### The research proposal

## INTRODUCTION

As was suggested in the first two chapters, the key to getting started on your dissertation is the production of a research proposal. It has three related and central rôles to play in the successful completion of the dissertation which are summarised below:

1 The preparation of a research proposal will force you to address what it is that you are actually hoping to achieve. Nothing focuses the mind more than having to write your thoughts down on paper. If the author had £1 for every student that had ever said 'I know what I want to do but just can't write it down,' he would be a wealthy man indeed. The standard reply to such a statement goes something like this, 'If you truly know what it is that you want to do, you *can* write it down. The only reason that you can't put any-

thing down in black and white is that you're not really sure what it is that you want to achieve.' Most people do however find that once they've set their initial ideas down on paper and read them over it make its considerably easier to then form a balanced judgement about whether their ideas are realistic ones. By 'realistic' is meant, 'Do the ideas have intellectual merit?' 'Am I going to risk overloading myself with the amount of work that will be needed to turn these ideas into a written dissertation within my time and resource constraints?', and so on. The sooner you get a research proposal finalised, the sooner you can get started. Remember, as noted in Chapter 1, procrastination is the thief of time. In the final analysis, sitting around just thinking about what you would like to do in your dissertation means that valuable days, weeks or even months (in the worst case) that could have been spent on improving the quality of your dissertation will have been lost forever. As Preece notes, 'Excessive delay in defining a topic in the early stages may lead to a failure to submit an adequate dissertation on time' (1994: 186).

2  Writing a research proposal allows your dissertation tutor to very quickly get a clear idea of your research purpose, the theoretical basis for your work, the chosen methods of investigation, etc. It is far easier for a tutor to give meaningful feedback to a dissertation student once ideas have been clearly set out in written form. Indeed, you may well find that your tutor is one of the many academic staff who will simply refuse to discuss dissertation ideas with students unless they've produced, at the very least, a brief written sketch of their initial thoughts.

3  Finally, as discussed at greater length later in the book, in undertaking any extensive piece of scholarly work such as a dissertation, there is always a need to regularly check oneself, to ensure that one is still on the right track. This is

especially so with inductive work. If you refer back to the plates, you can imagine that the inductive task of trying to impose some theoretical order on Plate 2 is a complex one. It is, for example, easy to get distracted by the cat, and go off down an avenue that leads you to draw conclusions about white cats, when it is really white balls of wool about which you wish to draw conclusions.

Although making the effort in the early part of the dissertation process to write a full and considered proposal may sometimes seem to be counter-productive, using up valuable time that could be spent instead on the main research endeavour, it will pay off handsomely in the long run. An hour spent clarifying that one wishes to draw conclusions about white wool rather than about white cats allows you to circumvent the possibility of spending two weeks researching white cats, which, interesting as it may be, is tangential to your true purpose. As de Vaus notes, 'It is tempting but inefficient to collect data before the research topic is clearly defined. This is highly inefficient since you normally end up collecting the wrong data' (de Vaus 1996: 27).

To conclude this introductory section, it is worth bearing in mind that the writing of proposals is not something that is confined to students. No matter how much research experience a scholar has, no matter how well regarded they are by their peers and no matter how small a sum of money they are seeking to support their endeavours, nothing will be forthcoming without a realistic and well-written proposal. As Black has noted, 'Very little, if any, respected research is totally unstructured and unplanned. Research does not just happen' (1993: 6). Moreover, when one thinks about it, doing research is really no different from any other type of activity. You would not expect your bank to lend to a new business that had not demonstrated its likely viability through a sound business plan. Few people would feel inclined to vote for a political party that stood on an electoral platform of, 'Vote for us, we'll tell you what our values and policies are once we're in power.' Getting your dissertation kick-started is about getting your own business plan organised, it is about producing your own manifesto. It is about writing a coherent research proposal.

## THE RESEARCH PROPOSAL 1: TOPIC CHOICE

If, as previously suggested, one fits method to problem and not vice versa, logically speaking topic choice has to be the first step in the dissertation process. This is also confirmed by looking at Bouma and Atkinson's discussion of getting started on the dissertation:

> *The first phase of the research process involves selecting a research problem, narrowing the focus of the question*, selecting a research design, defining and measuring variables, constructing an investigating instrument, and drawing a sample. *This phase is one of decision-making, sorting, narrowing, and clarifying. It requires clear thinking*. This means that favourite ideas and pet topics must be discarded for more precisely developed ideas.
>
> (Bouma and Atkinson 1995: 27, emphasis added)

To select a topic may sound straightforward and for some students it is. They have a clear and focused idea of what it is that they want to do. For those who are less sure how to go about choosing among a number of ideas, however, the process of topic choice can be a fairly painful one. If you find yourself in this position, there are a number of ways that you can move forward from a position that can, when you're in the middle of it, look like stalemate:

1 Decide which classes you have really enjoyed since beginning your degree. It may have been an advanced class or an

elementary class (although bear in mind that as advanced classes are more focused they are more likely to be fruitful as a source of dissertation ideas). Although this next point may sound obvious, do ensure that you select a core class and not something that you have studied as a 'filler'. You are, after all, going to be supervised and examined by people who are interested in political problems and will (with the notable exception of joint awards) be aiming to collect a degree in politics. Whilst there will almost certainly be scope for you to address a problem taken from, say, constitutional law or public sector economics, banish any thoughts that you may have of developing a dissertation out of the very interesting foundation class in psychology that you took in your first year. Moreover, although again this point seems obvious, you are cautioned against pursuing a subject where you have received marks that are lower than usual. If a certain subject has not been a strong point of yours in the past, don't assume that your abilities will miraculously improve by writing a dissertation in the field.

2  Although as noted above, 'favourite ideas and pet topics must be discarded' (Bouma and Atkinson 1995: 27), you can choose to build a dissertation around an investigation of a problem taken from personal experiences other than educational ones. For example, are you a member of a political party or a voluntary organisation? There will undoubtedly be political dissertation topics aplenty that can be developed out of such an area of personal interest. Do you play a sport? If you do, are there any angles relating to state regulation of or subsidy paid to that sport that you could develop into a dissertation? Although pet topics and personal hobby-horses are likely to interfere with the balance and judgement that is required of an academic piece of work, don't think that this rules out choosing problems from personal experience. As

noted in Chapter 1, at the end of the day the dissertation is a personal piece of work.

3   If your personal interests are, for example, limited to alcohol, tobacco and nightclubs, take time to look around the rich and problem-ridden world in which we live. There are any number of problems in this world of ours, and many of these will have a political component that is sufficiently clear to serve as the basis of a dissertation. Remember that dissertation ideas can come from 'an observation . . . a family crisis . . . a news report . . . a policy issue . . . ' (Bouma and Atkinson 1995: 28–9). By opening our eyes and ears we can find no end of problems to focus on. No less a person than the late Professor Sir Karl Popper passionately believed that it did not actually matter where a research idea came from, but whether or not it was any good (Popper 1980).

4   If you are still unsure about which topic to choose, you could always adopt the instrumental approach. That is, what do you hope to do after graduation? Can you do a dissertation that will help you to achieve your career goals? Although this is not really a sound academic basis for the choice of a dissertation topic, the thought of career advancement can certainly be useful in keeping your nose to the grindstone on those days that you'd rather watch television than get on with your dissertation.

5   Finally, although ideally you should be the one to choose your dissertation topic, if you have gone through steps 1 to 4 as noted above and find yourself still at a loss as to the way forward, ask people for help. Most public authorities will have problems that they're aware of but no staff time available to address them; politicians and political parties are always looking for people to do work for them on a voluntary basis; and last but not least, your dissertation tutor will be able to make suggestions. Check the notice-boards in your department too. A wide variety of voluntary

organisations put out calls for assistance, inviting students to contact them as they have an array of dissertation problems ready-formulated and awaiting solution.

Whatever your final choice of dissertation topic is, remember that both you and your dissertation tutor have to be happy with it. You – because this is a piece of work that will, as previously noted, stay with you for the remainder of your life, and your tutor – because they have the experience to know whether the topic that you propose to investigate is a suitable one.

## THE RESEARCH PROPOSAL 2: NARROWING AND CLARIFYING

Once you have identified a topic and agreed it with your tutor, you need to start to add focus to your study. As noted in Chapter 1, a relatively small number of students pursue dissertations that are entirely theoretical in nature. If you are one of these students, following your choosing of the topic you will need to 'unpack' it. The majority of students will however probably be planning to do a dissertation with both a theoretical and an empirical component. If you are one of these students, following your topic choice you will also need to unpack the topic, but in this instance as part and parcel of the process of *operationalisation* referred to previously. Remember that it is through operationalisation that you form the link between the theoretical and the empirical. Regardless of the type of dissertation that you plan to do however, the process of unpacking is absolutely central to the coherence of your work as it is unpacking that will, if done with due care and attention, add the much-needed *construct validity* to your work.

The literature proposes two main techniques for unpacking your topic and the technique that you choose ought to be informed by what you personally feel most comfortable with.

There is nothing particularly mysterious about these techniques: the first basically involves drawing simple box diagrams; the second drawing up bullet point lists. You need no special resources to unpack your topic, only a piece of paper, a pen or pencil and clarity of thought. Find yourself a block of quiet time to sit alone and start to unpack your topic, methodically working through the various permutations of what you can and cannot do in a dissertation that addresses your chosen topic. The whole process may involve spending a couple of hours to complete a first draft and it may be best to revisit your initial thoughts after an adequate period of reflection (a couple of days should suffice) and make suitable revisions to your unpacking as necessary. At the end of this simple process you should have added both the focus and the construct validity that your dissertation will need.

By way of demonstration, two worked examples are shown in Figure 3.1 and in Table 3.1 respectively. Figure 3.1 is an example of how one might unpack a topic chosen for a theoretical dissertation and Table 3.1 is an example of how one might unpack a topic chosen for a dissertation involving both the theoretical and the empirical. Do bear in mind that any type of dissertation topic can be unpacked using either technique. There is nothing to say, for example, that only theoretical problems can be unpacked by drawing box diagrams. The approach that you choose really ought not to be informed by anything other than your personal preference. If you like working with diagrams, work diagrammatically, if you don't like working with diagrams, don't.

Figure 3.1 shows an example of how you would go about unpacking a theoretical topic with the aid of a diagram. The key to producing such a diagram is clarity of thought. For instance, you can see at the top level that a decision has been made to pursue a dissertation that addresses a problem drawn from political theory. Political theory is however a huge field and, if a dissertation is to be sufficiently focused, there is a need to first unpack the broad field of political theory into smaller sub-fields, as shown at

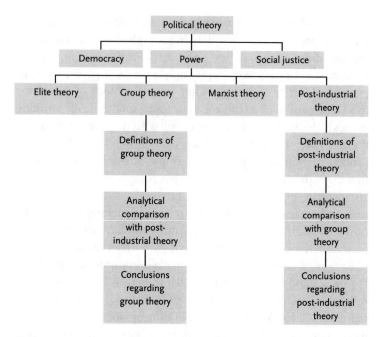

*Figure 3.1* Unpacking a theoretical dissertation topic using a diagram
*Source:* Adapted from de Vaus (1996: 52)

the second level. In this example only three options have been shown, but there are many others (for example there could easily be a box included at the second level for theories of the state).

As you read down the diagram the ideas are becoming more and more focused and if you were to draw such a diagram with sufficient care it would stand you in good stead for writing both your proposal and your dissertation. For instance, in writing a proposal based on Figure 3.1 you would seek first of all to provide a brief definition for and explanation of political theory. You would then go on to explain to the reader of the proposal that although you are very aware of the fact that political theory contains a wide variety of sub-fields, you are proposing to focus on power as opposed to democracy or social justice. You will then have to explain to the reader your *reasons* for choosing power as opposed to some other topic. In Figure 3.1 the theories of power have then been further unpacked, although once again the figure is illustrative only and could contain more boxes at the third level than the four that are shown (e.g. there could be a box for corporatist theories of power). Your next task is to explain to the reader why it is that you are proposing to focus on group theory and on post-industrial explanations of power. In other words, you will (as you did in discussing democracy and social justice) justify your choice, noting that while you are aware of other theoretical traditions, these two are the ones that you are most interested in exploring further. Moreover, trying to incorporate advanced analysis of all the available theoretical perspectives would simply not be possible within the confines of a dissertation. You would then go on in your proposal to say something about the means of data gathering and analysis (i.e. methods) that you propose to use as a basis for drawing valid conclusions about the problem in hand (again, note that methods are defined subsequently to the problem itself).

If properly constructed, the diagram should be able to be read either from top or bottom. For instance, if Figure 3.1 is read from the top it can be seen that what is being proposed is a political theory dissertation, addressing theories of power, within which special attention will be paid to group and post-industrial theories, that will be subjected to comparative analysis, as a means of drawing conclusions. On the other hand, if Figure 3.1 is read from bottom to top it can be seen that the aim of the proposed project is to draw conclusions from comparative analysis of the relative merits of group and post-industrial theories of power, with a view to producing a dissertation in the field of political theory. Regardless of the way that you look at any such diagram the purpose of your proposed study should be plain for all to see. Turning such a diagram into a proposal is relatively straightforward. In essence all that is required is a fleshed-out exposition of the diagram (the exposition will also contain limited reference to the literature) that talks the reader through the thought processes that led to its creation together with some comment on matters such as method and constraints. For further information on unpacking in this manner refer to de Vaus (1996) who has produced a similar diagram (but one that demonstrates how this particular unpacking technique can be applied in planning a piece of research that will involve linking the theoretical and the empirical).

Table 3.1 shows an example of how you would draw up a bullet point list to operationalise such a dissertation topic (i.e. one that will involve undertaking research that links the theoretical and the empirical). As with Figure 3.1, the key to this unpacking technique is again clarity of thought. Once you have decided what your chosen topic is, the next step according to Bouma and Atkinson (1995) is to ask yourself a range of pertinent questions about the topic concerned. For instance,

> Questions like the following may help to 'unpack' the topic:
>
> - What are the major concepts?
> - What is happening here?
> - What are the issues?
> - Is one thing affecting, causing, or producing a change in something else?
> - Why is this so?
>
> (Bouma and Atkinson 1995: 30)

In practice, by following this advice you will produce a bullet point list something akin to the one shown in Table 3.1

As you read down Table 3.1 the ideas are, as with the diagram example in Figure 3.1, becoming more and more focused. That is, at the top level, the topic chosen for dissertation study is

*Table 3.1* Operationalisation: unpacking from theoretical to empirical using bullets

| Topic | • Devolution and British central government |
| --- | --- |
| *What are the major concepts?* | • Democracy<br>• Decision-making<br>• Subsidiarity |
| *What is happening here?* | • Increase in democratic participation?<br>• Decrease in democratic participation?<br>• More efficient central government decision-making?<br>• Less efficient central government decision-making?<br>• Taking politics closer to the people?<br>• Power devolved is power retained? |
| *What are the issues?* | • Theoretical – devolved government will be closer to the people and encourage democratic participation |
| *Is one thing affecting, causing, or producing a change in something else?* | • Empirical – has there been a change in the percentage of people registered to vote? Has there been a change in the percentage of electors voting in elections (e.g. European, Westminster, devolved and local)? Any change in the percentage of people who're members of parties? etc. |
| *Why is this so?* | • Has the theory's prediction been supported by the empirical data? If yes, was the data gathered valid, reliable and representative? If no, why was the prediction wrong? |

*Source:* Based on Bouma and Atkinson (1995)

shown as, 'devolution and British central government'. This topic has then been unpacked into a range of relevant constituent concepts (democracy, decision-making and subsidiarity, although as with Figure 3.1 there could well be many more bullet points listed here). At the next level, it can be seen that a decision has been made in this example to focus the proposed study on issues of democratic participation as opposed to those on the efficiency of decision-making or on the extent to which the principles of subsidiarity have been realised.

Note that these first three steps have dealt with theoretical unpacking, in much the same manner as Figure 3.1 did. The main difference between the theoretical dissertation and one that aims to address the link between the theoretical and empirical worlds can be seen in levels four and five of Table 3.1. The operationalisation, linking together the theoretical and empirical, is once again a product of clear thinking. You can see from Table 3.1 that the dissertation proposed here is a deductive one. In other words, as previously noted in Table 1.3, 'the research progresses from the adoption of a theoretical position and the prediction of what ought to be found in the empirical world if the theory is a good analogue of that empirical world. The researcher will then proceed to investigate the empirical world in which they find both themselves and their problem in order to test the theory and to draw conclusions about its explanatory value.' Consistent with this deductive approach, the fourth level of Table 3.1 sets forth a theoretical proposition, in this case that, 'devolved government will be closer to the people and encourage democratic participation'. The fifth level of Table 3.1 completes the operationalisation process, setting forth a range of empirical factors that could be investigated to test the theoretical proposition. The sixth level of Table 3.1 sets out the final stage of a deductive study that links together the theoretical and the empirical, i.e. draws conclusions about the theory's explanatory value.

If logically unpacked, the bullet point list of Table 3.1 should, as was the case with Figure 3.1, be capable of being read either from top or bottom without causing the reader confusion. Once again you will find that turning such a list of bullet points into a proposal is fairly straightforward. In this instance all that is required is a fleshed-out exposition of the bullet points (again including limited reference to the literature). For further information on unpacking in this manner refer to Bouma and Atkinson (1995) who have produced other worked examples. Moreover, as previously noted, this unpacking technique can be applied just as effectively in planning a piece of research that is entirely theoretical in nature.

Whichever unpacking technique you prefer, taking the time to sit quietly and think through exactly what it is that you want to do in a structured fashion will benefit your endeavours enormously. The following piece of advice cannot be repeated too many times: the clearer and more focused your problem the better your prospects of success. *This cannot be overemphasised.* In the author's experience the majority of students find it very useful to focus their problem by unpacking their chosen topic, by using a diagram or bullet points, regardless of whether their aim is to link the theoretical with the empirical or to stick with the theoretical alone. To summarise the process of getting started on a research proposal then:

1 Identify a topic.
2 Unpack the topic into its component parts.
3 Narrow down to focus on only one or two of these component parts.
4 Start to think about what type of information you'll need to gather and how you're going to gather and analyse it.
5 Think about whether the work that you are proposing will allow you to draw valid conclusions that will have relevance within the framework of your chosen topic. If not, something has gone wrong with the unpacking. Remember, if your unpacking has been logical there should be a clear and logical thread linking your conclusions back to your topic. If, at the end of your unpacking process this looks unlikely,

you are advised to do the unpacking again. Better to spend another two hours re-doing your unpacking at this stage than to spend a year researching and writing a dissertation only to discover that your examiner fails to see a clear and logical link between your intentions and your conclusions. Remember, *construct validity* is of central importance in any dissertation and it is through the unpacking/operationalisation process that your work will be ensured of this.

## THE RESEARCH PROPOSAL 3: GOING TO THE LIBRARY

Once you have finished unpacking your chosen topic, you are nearly, but not quite ready to write your proposal. Bear in mind that although the unpacking ought to imbue your proposal with *construct* validity, your work will need to display *content* validity also. The simplest way in which you can add this type of validity to your proposal is by making clear reference to sources drawn from the academic literature (that is, as long as you can show that these sources are indeed relevant to your proposed study). Although Chapter 4 will be given over to discussion of undertaking the literature review for your dissertation itself, you will need to undertake a limited literature review before you can complete your proposal. You do not need to undertake an extensive review of the literature in order to prepare a proposal, as this is, after all, part and parcel of doing the dissertation proper. Furthermore, if you've chosen a topic about which you already have some knowledge it shouldn't be too difficult for you to track down the sources that you need. Although it varies depending on the topic, you wouldn't normally need to refer to more than about a dozen sources to write a proposal.

Making reference to the literature serves a number of purposes. Most importantly it demonstrates content validity to the reader, but there are other associated benefits:

1  It will certainly help you to pick up on any nuances of the topic chosen for investigation that you might have missed in your unpacking.

2  If you have chosen a topic on the basis of a class that you have previously taken, the nature of the topic might have changed slightly since you took that class. Remember that a week is a long time in politics. While you are unlikely to suffer from this sort of problem to the same extent if your focus is primarily theoretical, the sands of the empirical world shift on a daily basis. Undertaking a cursory review of the current literature will ensure that your problem is still relevant in its unpacked form.

3  A brief review of the literature will let you know whether your early thoughts regarding the methods of investigation have sufficient merit for you to proceed henceforth.

Following on from the unpacking then, a brief literature review is an essential part of defining the problem. Before you finally sit down to write your research proposal there is every chance that you will find yourself further refining your unpacking as a consequence of your reading. Indeed, once you have chosen your topic, completed your initial unpacking, reviewed your initial thoughts, undertaken a brief literature review and reviewed your unpacking again, you should be able to state with clarity the nature of your research problem, i.e. write your research proposal.

Do, however, make sure that you choose your topic and unpack it first. When you work in this fashion you automatically set yourself boundaries for the brief literature review. Working in the other direction, i.e. looking to the literature in the first instance, often causes confusion and proves counter-productive. There is no point engaging in an extended search of the library shelves and a massive liteature review in the early stages. All that this tends to do is muddy the conceptual waters. Remember, clarity of purpose comes from within your own mind far more than it does from sources which are external to it (i.e. books, journals, etc.). Get your internal thought processes working first and then build upon and criticise these thoughts by making reference to the relevant materials. Further information on literature searching and review in the dissertation itself forms the basis for the next chapter.

## THE RESEARCH PROPOSAL 4: WRITING YOUR PROPOSAL

If you have followed through the advice presented within this chapter, you are now in a position to write your proposal. As ever, you may find that your department has a set or preferred format for the writing of proposals. If it does, then follow the departmental format. Again, where there is conflict between the department's preferred format and the one that will be suggested below, stick with the former. Although there are 'wrong' ways to write a proposal there is not really a 'right' way. There are always going to be several 'right' ways. Most dissertation tutors will be willing to accept thoughtful deviation from the preferred format, but do not go out of your way to challenge the established orthodoxy. You have bigger fish to fry. Keep your energy reserves for the dissertation itself and, whatever else you do, keep in mind at all times that the more focused your problem the better.

How long should a proposal be? Again, look to your departmental guidance. As a rough indication, however, a proposal of about 2,500 words will generally manage to cover everything that's necessary in sufficient depth. These will not be wasted words either; very often students manage to recycle most of their proposal in the introductory stages of the dissertation itself. Regardless of the length or structure of your proposal do ensure that you demonstrate to the reader: (1) that you understand your chosen topic; (2) that your proposed study is ethical; (3) that you have thought about issues of reliability, validity and representativeness; and (4) that the work can be done within the constraints. Remember that even if you are in the fortunate position of having plenty of time and money, you may still be constrained. Will you be able to access the information you need easily? For instance, will the holders of the information be willing to provide access to it, will all the requisite literature be available in a language known to you, etc.?

You also ought by now to have given some thought as to whether your problem will be best addressed by qualitative means, quantitative means or by some combination of these. You must be able to provide a justification in your research proposal for the methodological approach that you wish to adopt in addressing your problem. You are of course advised to justify this choice of method by making reference to the appropriate academic literature.

You are now ready to sit down and write your proposal. If you have followed all of the steps suggested in this chapter you may well be pleasantly surprised at how quickly you can get 2,500 words (or however many are required) down on paper. This will simply be the reward for the amount of preparatory work that you have put in so far.

Above all else your research proposal should be structured logically. If your department has a template for preparing a proposal, use it. On the other hand, if you are free to structure your proposal in your own way, the structure shown in Table 3.2 should cover most of the points that you'll need to address before getting on to your dissertation proper. Please do note, though, that this is only a suggested and not a prescribed structure. A prescribed structure has not been offered here because, as with choice of method, the structure of both the proposal and the dissertation will depend to a certain extent on the nature of your topic and indeed on personal preference. As Table 3.2 shows, the suggestion is for you to structure your proposal in a ten-step process.

Finally, in presenting your research proposal, try using the layout that you will later adopt for your dissertation itself. Once again, your dissertation tutor will be able to provide you with guidance on presentation. Issues of particular relevance include the referencing style to be adopted (it is suggested here that the Harvard referencing system is the easiest to use in a longer piece of work – note for example that it has been used in this volume), and the format to which the final typed dissertation should conform. If your department doesn't have guidelines then you could do worse than to set your proposal and your dissertation out as follows: use white A4/letter size paper, with pages printed on one side only and consecutively numbered; adopt a left hand margin of 40 mm(to allow for binding), with all other margins being 15 mm); ensure one and a half or double spaced text (except for indented quotes, footnotes, etc.) in 11 or 12 point type, avoiding fancy fonts.

To conclude this section of the chapter you ought now to be in a position to complete your research proposal. Once you have completed a sound proposal and this has been seen and agreed with your dissertation tutor you are ready to get started on the dissertation itself. As emphasised at the start of this chapter, be tempted to dispense with the proposal and proceed directly with the dissertation *at your own peril*.

You may of course eventually find that your dissertation does not end up quite as you had planned it. This is not a major problem; nobody will penalise you if a major upset has occurred within your chosen field as your work progresses or if you haven't managed for good reasons to collect all of the data that you'd hoped to or if you've changed your theoretical slant somewhat as a result of doing the dissertation. This is simply part and parcel of academic work, whether it is in the field of politics or in any other subject.

As far as further reading is concerned, unfortunately, the art of writing a good research proposal is a commercially valuable one

*Table 3.2* Suggestions for structuring a research proposal

| Step | Suggestion |
| --- | --- |
| 1 | Choose your dissertation topic using the suggestions made in Chapter 3 |
| 2 | Unpack your topic as suggested in Chapter 3. Review and revise unpacking |
| 3 | Do a brief literature review of relevance to your topic. Review unpacking again |
| 4 | Write your 'rationale'. This section is the key to a focused proposal and will serve to direct the dissertation itself. Essentially a short essay, the rationale will lead to a clear statement of what your research aims are rather than to its solution. It involves working in the opposite direction from normal, i.e. you will be ending up with a question rather than starting with one. Word your text around the structure that you've adopted in the unpacking, talking readers through the unpacking process, showing them why you propose to address your topic and how. Remember to make reference to the literature to demonstrate your acquaintance with it. The rationale is an academic justification that forms the basis of your dissertation. It may use up to half the proposal's word limit |
| 5 | At the end of the rationale you should be able to set down a clearly defined statement of the research problem and, where appropriate, either a hypothesis or detailed aims and objectives. The choice of hypothesis or aims will depend largely on what type of problem it is that you are addressing. Further information is provided on hypotheses, aims and objectives in Chapters 5 and 6. If in doubt as to which format is most appropriate for your problem, ask your tutor |
| 6 | Return to the literature and review your thoughts on method |

*Table 3.2* – contd

| | |
|---|---|
| 7 | Following on from the clear statement of your research problem and statement of hypothesis or aims, write a section in which you explain the methods that you choose to employ in addressing your problem. Remember to cover all the methods that you plan to use at all stages of the work (e.g. in the literature review, in gathering empirical information, in analysis, etc.) and to make appropriate reference to the literature when writing this section up |
| 8 | Provide a section that includes information on the time and resource constraints as you see them and a plan of how you will allocate your time and resources. Include a list of anticipated outcomes in this section e.g. X will be achieved by the end of month one, Y will be achieved by the end of month two, etc. |
| 9 | Ensure that you append a bibliography and check over your proposal to ensure that it has been adequately referenced throughout |
| 10 | Write an abstract to go at the front of the proposal that summarises the entire piece for the reader's benefit. You will almost certainly have to include one in your dissertation, so if you haven't prepared one before, it is worth practising. If you're unsure what an abstract looks like, pick up any academic journal. You will find an abstract at the top of every paper in most journals. Try to keep the abstract to 100–200 words (it is after all a summary) |

(indeed it is one of the few tools of the academic trade that is undoubtedly of significant commercial value). The word 'unfortunately' is used here as the commercial value means that most of the people who are skilled in writing proposals like to keep the secrets of success to themselves. In a competitive world, why share your knowledge of how to write a good proposal with everyone else? At the end of the day the consequence of this could well be sharing your research funding with others. In terms of further reading, you are also warned to be aware that many of the other texts available on planning and writing dissertations are more likely to have been written with sociology and/ or psychology students in mind than politics students, and that most of them are pitched at a higher (PhD) level. Thus other texts can give an unrealistic expectation of what is required of you as an undergraduate student writing a dissertation in politics. That is not to denigrate these sources in any way – most of them are very good – it is just to note that few have been written with you in mind. Provided you take this warning on board, you could gain valuable advice from the following: Bell (1999); Blaxter et al. (1996); Bouma and Atkinson (1995); Cryer (2000); Preece (1994); Rudestam and Newton (2000).

Finally, above all else remember that your endeavours in undertaking a dissertation will be made easier by maintaining focus at all times. As Black notes of professional academic research, 'most published research in journals tends to result from reasonable, limited statements of research intent' (1993: 26). In Chapter 4 the first step in the process that will lead to the dissertation proper will be examined, namely the literature review.

## SUMMARY

From this chapter we may conclude:

1 that all academic research should be based on a proposal;
2 that the preparation of a proposal encourages clarity in your own thoughts and purpose;
3 that the preparation of a proposal is the most effective way of demonstrating the merit of your ideas to your dissertation tutor;
4 that a solid proposal will serve as a guide that will keep you on track as your dissertation progresses;

5  that there are several easy ways in which you can choose a realistic topic;
6  that you can quickly and easily add construct validity to a theoretical dissertation through logical unpacking;
7  that you can quickly and easily form an operational link between the theoretical and empirical worlds through logical unpacking;
8  that you can quickly and easily add content validity to your research proposal through a limited but focused review of relevant literature;
9  that a robust research proposal can be produced as the result of following an easy ten-step process; and
10 that the more focused your personal problem the better your prospects of success in writing your dissertation.

## TEST YOUR KNOWLEDGE OF THIS CHAPTER

Please refer to p. 19 for details.

# 4

## REFINING THE PROBLEM

### The literature review

## INTRODUCTION

Once you have defined and justified your research problem in a coherent and structured fashion through the mechanism of the research proposal, you are ready to begin work on your dissertation proper. The first step in your dissertation research will normally be to undertake a thorough and methodical review of the relevant literature (i.e. within the boundaries of your problem as defined in the proposal). In preparing essays etc. since you started your degree you should have become more and more adept at searching for and reviewing literature beyond the confines of the basic reading lists that you have been given by your tutors. As a consequence, this is a fairly brief chapter which assumes that you have already developed many or indeed most of the skills that you will need to undertake the literature review that will almost certainly end up forming a key part of your dissertation.

The literature review is the foundation for your dissertation. Although you may read elsewhere of research models that do not start off with a literature review (they do exist) such models are generally inapplicable as far as writing a dissertation is concerned. The author is not personally aware of the existence of any departments that would encourage candidates to submit a dissertation that lacked a thorough review of relevant literature. Admittedly such departments may exist, it is just that the author is not aware of any (indeed, if any reader does know of such a department – in the United Kingdom at least – please get in touch and let the author know). Thus, assuming that most departments will want their dissertation students to submit a final piece that includes a review of literature, this chapter's advice will be of relevance to nearly all readers, regardless of what they plan to investigate and regardless of how they plan to do it.

*The literature review will allow you to build on and refine your proposal ideas* (hence the title of this chapter). Indeed, although you will find that the activity of reviewing literature will be ongoing throughout the process of researching and writing the dissertation, it is customary to spend a considerable time on this activity *before* getting stuck into the business of gathering and analysing data. One of the clearest justifications for so doing (and one which has resonance both theoretically and practically) is this – if your ideas are likely to be refined as a result of a thorough review of the literature, it is perfectly plausible that your data requirements, the finer detail of your proposed method, etc. will also need to be refined.

Assuming that you have learned the basics of how to use a library by the time you come to read this book, you will find that self-discipline, focus and clarity of thought will be the keys to assuring the quality of your literature review. Remember that unlike many of the other pieces of work that you have done in the past there is no set question and no reading list. You were in charge of setting your own question in the proposal and you will also be in charge of building your own reading list for the literature review. When building this reading list you must, as ever, retain focus. The practical effect of being focused is that you cannot expect to get away with reading lots of basic chapters in basic textbooks. If you have used this approach in the past to write essays bear in mind (as shown in Chapter 1) that, 'in addressing the essay or examination question you will have read around the syllabus with a view to answering questions that are, in comparison with a dissertation, fairly broad'. Consequently, while basic textbooks will find a place in any review of literature, it will be a limited one. The focus and depth that is required of you will mean that your review of literature needs to draw to a far greater extent on advanced texts and on academic journal articles than would be needed in writing an average essay.

To finish this introductory section, then, the advice is to remember the need for focus. The reason that you were advised to prepare a research proposal in Chapter 3 was to limit the scope of your investigations. Do not then, in undertaking the literature review, proceed to read and read and read without due regard to this focus. If, half-way through reading a source, you come to the conclusion that this source is unlikely to be of much value in addressing your problem, put it down and pick something else up instead. You are under no obligation to finish reading everything that you've started; to do so is wasteful in terms of time and effort and where materials are not of direct relevance they can in fact distract you from your purpose. Be self-disciplined and think clearly. With reference back to the plates, if it is white balls of wool rather than white cats that you're focusing on, make sure that you don't spend a month reading about white cats.

## WHAT THE LITERATURE REVIEW IS AND WHAT IT IS NOT

The literature review serves a number of purposes as far as the successful completion of an academic dissertation in politics is concerned. Although it will be more central to some dissertations than to others (as ever this will depend in no small part upon the nature of your problem; seek advice from your tutor if in doubt) the following five points are pretty much pertinent to all dissertations. That is, the literature review will help you to:

1  gain an in-depth feel for your topic, i.e. regarding both its historical roots and current theory;
2  further refine the nature of your research problem as set out in your proposal (not least by giving you an idea of what has and what has not been done before, thereby giving you food for thought regarding the detailed nature of your chosen problem);
3  add scholarly weight and content validity to the written output that you will eventually produce – someone who is well acquainted with the literature is more likely to be taken seriously by examiners;
4  judge whether the methods that you had in mind when preparing your proposal need to be refined – in reading other authors' methodological justifications you may feel it appropriate to further refine your own thoughts on method; and
5  make sense of your findings when the time comes to undertake your analysis – for instance, completing a thorough literature review will enable you to draw conclusions about whether your findings are commensurate with or at odds with the findings of others.

Taking these five points into consideration, it is now worthwhile clarifying exactly what a literature review is and what it isn't. If you refer to Table 4.1 you will see that a schematic synopsis has been provided here for your reference. Unfortunately the term 'literature review' can mean different things to different people and one consequence of this is that there is not an established definition that is used consistently in textbooks. Thus, with reference to point 5 above, you would, if you were to conduct research into what a literature review is, come to the conclusion

*Table 4.1* Some thoughts on what a literature review is – and is not

| A literature review is | A literature review is not |
| --- | --- |
| Something that will help you to refine the problem that you established through the rationale in your research proposal | A primary means of defining your problem. Look back to Chapter 3 for further information on this |
| A means of addressing issues of relevance to the research problem that arise out of the literature (as guided by the research proposal) | A compendium of abstracts relating to everything that has ever been written on a topic. An academic literature review is focused according to research aims |
| One of the first tasks to be undertaken by the dissertation student | A task that is limited to only the early part of the research |
| Critical and analytical, addressing the merit of written works as well as summarising their contents | A purely descriptive exercise. The purpose of an academic literature review is to examine arguments, not catalogue them |
| Of necessity, an activity that involves reference to *academic* sources, e.g. even today using the internet as your sole source is unlikely to suffice | By any means restricted to discussion of ideas emerging from the academic literature alone. Websites, newspaper reports, etc. can all be included |

that the definition offered in Table 4.1 is not entirely commensurate with the definitions of others.

Over and above the definition in Table 4.1 of what a literature review is and is not, the reader ought to bear in mind two further comments. *In the first instance, although a dissertation can be based entirely on analysis of printed materials that does not mean that the resultant dissertation is simply a large literature review.* Look back to the five explanatory points listed earlier in this chapter. There is a distinction to be drawn between refining your problem, refining your method and setting the scene (literature review) and the process of generating findings from the detailed examination of printed materials. (This process will be identified by the term 'documentary analysis' throughout the remainder of this volume.) This distinction is of particular relevance to political dissertations as these can often be heavily reliant upon analysis of printed matter. Further discussion of documentary analysis as a method of research is to be found in Chapters 5 and 6.

*Second, do not fall into the common trap of confusing the dissertation that is based on literature review plus documentary analysis with the theoretical dissertation.* For instance, a student sitting in Australia could, given access to the right information, produce an outstanding dissertation on some political issue in South Africa. Given that the student concerned is unlikely to visit South Africa, however, their information may well come entirely in a printed format. Hence, although the work would be based on literature review plus documentary analysis it would not be a purely theoretical dissertation in so far as it addresses political issues from the empirical world. The theoretical dissertation is, admittedly, a dissertation based on literature review plus documentary analysis, but not all such dissertations are theoretical in nature.

## DOING THE LITERATURE REVIEW

By now, you should have a research proposal that has been agreed with your dissertation tutor and a clearer idea of what a literature review is and is not. It is now nearly time to settle yourself down in the library (or wherever else you find that you can work) and get reviewing. Before you do so however, give some thought to the techniques that you will use to find the sources that you need. As noted earlier you ought by now to know how to use a library, so extensive discussion of the basics will not be offered here. Rather, take as a starting point the shelfmarks of those sources that you had consulted in preparing your proposal and spend some time browsing for relevant books there. Then go to the journal stocks and identify the titles that will be of relevance to you (students are often surprised by the number that they find). Most importantly of all though, let your search for materials be guided by your research aims as set down in your proposal. Remember, reading about white cats does not tell you anything about white balls of wool. Once you've spent some time acquainting yourself with the library stock (both books and journals) you are then ready to get started in earnest. While your literature review is progressing, above all else work in a style that feels comfortable. Sometimes people like to take all their notes first, reflect upon them and then sit down to write the review itself. Others prefer to write the review as they go. You have been a student long enough now to know what works for you; stick with it. In terms of practical advice however, find below ten suggestions for ensuring that your review of literature is as efficient and effective as possible, no matter how you execute it in detail.

1 Ask people who are working in the same field for a list of key references. These people may include your dissertation tutor, other staff in your institution (not necessarily the same department) and people external to your institution.

2   Use local libraries in the first instance. It is self-evident that this will save you time and money (although see also point 6 below). If you are fortunate enough to be studying in a location where there is more than one institution of higher education, go and check out the library of the 'other place(s)'. Different staff purchase different books and journals and you may find the most important source of all hiding on the shelves of the 'other place'. If you think that you will need to use the library of another institution on a regular basis, consider taking out membership as an external reader if you can afford it (the prices are usually fairly reasonable for students, although deposits can sometimes be hefty). If you haven't already done so, join your local public library too. Although the standards of public library provision are variable (depending in large part on political priorities and budget setting) they can be very good. For instance, despite recent cuts, the standard of public library provision in the author's home city is very good in comparison with many other places, owing to the political commitment of the Aberdeen City Council to public library services.

3   Use these local libraries to their full extent: refer to the subject index to find out about shelfmarks that you haven't yet looked at (not forgetting to check reference and short loan collections); refer to collections of abstracts, indexes and citation indexes, making full use of CD versions where you have access to them and are confident in using them; refer to bibliographies (e.g. the British National Bibliography, Bookbank) and, if your institution subscribes, make use of the *Bath Information and Data Services* (commonly known as *BIDS* and found at <http://www.bids.ac.uk/>) through which you will be able to access bibliographic databases as well as electronic journals; and, when looking through the academic journals, make sure to check either

the last or the first issue in any volume. Finally, you will find that most journals publish an index of all the articles that have recently been published in that journal in one of these issues. Getting hold of the issue that contains the index saves a lot of work.

4  If any of the terms used in point 3 above are ones that you are not acquainted with seek assistance from the library staff who will be able to explain them to you on an individual basis. If you choose to approach the librarians at a quiet time of day and do so in a polite manner you may find that you are pleasantly surprised by their knowledge and expertise. Use this expertise to your own advantage – surprisingly few students do.

5  Where you are searching for materials that were printed some time ago, remember that they may well be stored in a condensed format. Nowadays such materials are most often stored on CD but you may still find some on microfiche or microfilm. Again, ask the library staff for assistance.

6  If you wish to access specialist material that is not available locally, speak to the library staff about inter-library loans. You may find that you are charged for these (especially if you need them quickly) and even if you aren't, be aware that there will probably be a limit as to how many you can request before you are asked to pay. Indeed, if you should find yourself investigating a topic that will involve a lot of inter-library loans it may be both faster and cheaper for you to go to the material than to request that it comes to you. In the United Kingdom it may pay off to visit one of the 'legal deposit libraries' (which stock copies of all books, journals, etc. published in the UK as well as materials from overseas). Each of the UK's four constituent nations has one and you can use them if you get a member of academic staff to sign the relevant application form (again ask your local library staff for further details). Furthermore, you will find

that research institutes, legislatures, central government departments, local authorities, quangos, political parties, pressure groups and newspapers all have their own specialist libraries which they will sometimes let people use (although they are not necessarily under an obligation to do so). The key to access, as ever, is politeness.

7 Remember to look beyond books and journals. News-papers, parliamentary proceedings and legislation can all be of direct relevance to the student of politics. Moreover, most libraries will also hold a wealth of resources such as reports, monographs and occasional papers, conference proceedings, dissertations, etc. Do take great care when using such works however. As will be discussed in conclud-ing this chapter, many of these will be categorised as 'unpublished work' and as such you may not be able to quote from them (or even cite them in some instances).

8 The internet continues to develop in its usefulness as a source of information and can be especially invaluable for downloading large amounts of text-based information from overseas. For example, in the United Kingdom it is almost impossible to get hold of American statutes in printed form. That said, more often than not you can download the one that you want from the US Library of Congress website. As previously noted in Table 4.1, however, 'even today using the internet as your sole source is unlikely to suffice'. Pub-lishing on the internet is not subject to quality control in the same way as academic journals and commercially published books are. Be wary of internet sources and use your com-mon sense. It is fine to use a policy statement taken from the website of a government department but unacceptable to rely on a statement taken from the James Dobson homepage or such like.

9 Every time that you review a source, be sure and check the footnotes, references, bibliography, etc. This is undoubtedly

one of the quickest and easiest ways to get further information on reading matter relevant to your topic.

10  Finally, it makes sense to purchase a copy of anything that is going to be truly central to your studies. This avoids the problem of having texts recalled by the library. Furthermore, it is also often possible to get copies of political documents without charge, whether they be published by political parties, governmental or non-governmental organisations. Where this is the case, take a minute to make a request by telephone or e-mail for a copy. Once again this means that you will always have your own copy of the document to hand and will not be left cursing at a recall notice issued by the library.

## WILL I COPE?

You may have come to the conclusion in reading the previous section that doing a literature review may not be quite as straightforward a task as you'd first imagined. Indeed, when one takes time to read through a variety of the materials that have been written on the reviewing of literature, a number of problems might be encountered by the reviewer are commonly identified. These potential problems are usefully summarised in the bullet point list taken from Blaxter et al. (1996: 94–5):

- *The volume of literature.* The amount of material written on most subjects is already huge, and expanding at an ever increasing rate. How does the researcher get to grips with this?

- *The variety of literature.* There are so many kinds of literature (e.g. textbooks, journals, magazines, newspapers, policy documents, academic papers, conference papers, internal reports, novels, etc.) which may be relevant. How does the researcher use this range of sources?

- *Lack of boundaries.* Unless a project is very tightly defined, it may be impossible to judge which areas of the literature are relevant. How does the researcher avoid reading too widely or aimlessly?
- *Conflicting arguments.* As soon as you start reading, you are likely to be confronted by different opinions, arguments and interpretations. It may seem that no two writers agree about even the most basic issues. How do researchers assess these arguments, and place themselves within them?

However, this author sincerely believes that if students have prepared a thoughtful and realistic research proposal, if they take account of the tips given in this chapter and proceed to undertake their review with focus and self-discipline in a manner with which they feel comfortable, there should be no major problems. Look again at the four issues raised by Blaxter *et al.* (1996). Your proposal should determine sufficiently clear boundaries and these boundaries should in turn help you to manage the volume of material. As far as managing the variety of material and assessing conflicting arguments are concerned, how did you get to the stage of writing a dissertation without having mastered these skills? To conclude this section, then, don't worry unduly – you'll cope. Indeed, the only thing that is likely to cause you any real difficulty is structuring the review of literature when you come to write it up. As Cuba and Cocking have noted:

> it is probably fair to say that literature reviews demand more of their writers than other forms of writing. They involve a familiarity with a larger quantity of research and require more exacting skills of selection, classification and critical analysis. In many ways literature reviews are exercises in comparative writing.
>
> (Cuba and Cocking 1994: 54)

The issues of the comparative method will be explored in greater detail in Chapter 7. As far as issues of structure are concerned, however, it is to these that we will turn our attention next.

## STRUCTURING YOUR WRITTEN REVIEW OF LITERATURE

Despite their words of warning Cuba and Cocking (1994) go on to give excellent advice regarding the approaches to structure that can be adopted when writing your literature review. For example:

> Literature reviews are usually organised either *topically* or *chronologically*; most frequently they are structured *topically*. In such cases previous research is divided into segments representing conceptual subsets of some larger issue. For example, a review of a concept like alienation, which has identifiable dimensions, may be logically organised in the light of these dimensions, i.e., powerlessness, meaninglessness, or normlessness.
>
> (Cuba and Cocking 1994: 57)

You can regard the above as being sound advice, advice which is echoed throughout the generality of writings on reviewing literature. This is not to say that the chronological structure does not have a place, however. As usual, the nature of the review's structure will depend on the nature of the problem in hand. For example, if you imagine a topic such as the politics of privatisation during Margaret Thatcher's second government, it would make eminent sense to start your review in 1983 and work forwards to 1987. Students can also usefully employ a mixture of the topical and the chronological. For instance, it is perfectly reasonable to write a topical review with a chronological sub-structure employed in discussion of the separate topics (or vice versa). If you are unclear as to which structure is most appropriate for you to adopt, consult your dissertation tutor, they will be able to advise you. As long as the structure employed is one that allows you to effectively set the scene for your detailed investigations in a logical and ordered fashion, all will be well. If you want to read more about the structuring of literature reviews you are directed again towards Cuba and Cocking (1994) where you will find excellent advice. To conclude this chapter, however, do pay attention to the following dangers when undertaking your literature review:

1   The literature review is important, but is an activity which will not in its own right lead to the production of a finished dissertation alone. Some people tend to get 'stuck' when reviewing the literature and continue to do so long after they have ceased to derive benefit from it. In large part this is because they have become used to reading for essays and examinations and are daunted by starting work on the other tasks that they will have to undertake in order to complete their dissertation on time (where these other tasks form the subject matter of Chapters 5, 6, 7 and 8). If you catch yourself falling into this trap, pick up any basic text on economics and review the law of diminishing returns.

2   As previously noted, when reviewing certain types of material you may be restricted by copyright laws if you wish to quote from them, and in some instances even from referring to them. Wherever and whenever you are writing your dissertation, make sure that you are aware of the copyright laws that apply to you. Once more, library staff can often offer helpful advice in this regard. As a general rule however you are best not to quote from work which is in progress or from other people's dissertations. Additionally, if you plan to use an exceptionally large quotation it is good practice to ask the holder of the copyright for permission beforehand. Finally, it is best to assume that you can

*never* make an exact reproduction of diagrams or photographs without explicit permission. The only exception may be where the publication from which you are extracting the material has a blanket exemption. Nevertheless, even where such an exemption exists, it often applies only to the text (and less often diagrams also). Take care and remember that you are better off safe than sorry. As established in Chapter 2, you wish to undertake your research in a manner that is ethical and this does imply staying within the relevant legal confines.

Finally, for further reading, Cuba and Cocking (1994) has already been highly recommended. Other sources to which you can make reference for further developing your knowledge of literature reviews include: Babbie (1995); Bell (1999); Blaxter *et al.* (1996); Bouma and Atkinson (1995); Creswell (1994).

## SUMMARY

From this we may conclude:

1 that the literature review is an essential part of the dissertation;
2 that the review of literature is started early in the dissertation process but will continue throughout it;
3 that the literature review is useful in further refining your research aims as set out in your proposal;
4 that the literature review is useful in further refining your thoughts on method as set out in your proposal;
5 that there is a distinction to be drawn between literature reviewing and documentary analysis;
6 that literature and theory are not one and the same;
7 that there are a number of entirely practical measures that

you can take to improve the efficiency and effectiveness of your reviewing of literature;

8 that the structure of your literature review should be determined by the nature of your problem;

9 that care needs to be taken regarding copyright law when reviewing certain categories of literature; and

10 that you will, through your studies to date, already have developed most of the skills needed to successfully complete a focused review of the relevant literature, guided by your research proposal.

## TEST YOUR KNOWLEDGE OF THIS CHAPTER

Please refer to p. 19 for details.

# 5

## DEDUCTION, QUANTIFICATION AND THE EMPIRICAL DISSERTATION

### Facing up to feline frolics

## INTRODUCTION

As explained in the preface to this book, its overall purpose is not to provide detailed training in the finer points of research methods, either quantitative or qualitative. There are a great many books available to which you can refer if you are interested in undertaking a quantitative project for your dissertation that will ultimately rely upon your having developed a thorough working understanding of content analysis or of linear regression techniques. For instance Pennings *et al.* (1999) deal with both. It is decidedly *not* the purpose of this book to even attempt to cover the wide range of quantitative techniques that are available to the social scientist and no apology is made for that.

Readers will be directed to further reading throughout this chapter, but you ought to have no difficulties in accessing the acres of material that have been produced on quantitative social research. A visit to the library to inspect the stocks held at the shelfmarks for social research and statistics should serve to confirm this assertion. Thus, what this chapter sets out to achieve is to put down some key markers for the student interested in doing a dissertation that addresses political issues from the empirical world, through the employment of quantitative means. Chapter 6 will set out to do the same for qualitative means. To reiterate then, this chapter should not be read as a definitive statement on the quantitative tradition – it isn't. There are so many authoritative sources available to the interested dissertation student that it would be pointless to simply repeat that which you will find expressed better elsewhere. This chapter's purpose is instead simply to address a range of the fundamental issues that anyone undertaking quantitative work for their dissertation will face and to make suggestions on how to ensure that this work is executed in as efficient and as painless a fashion as possible.

Prior to addressing this subject matter it is pertinent to note that, as stated in Chapter 2, you do not need to be a mathematical wizard to undertake a solid quantitative study. You do, however, have to take care that you operate within your own boundaries regarding the application of numerical techniques. If you have taken classes in quantitative methods and have developed competence with more advanced techniques, feel free to use these in your dissertation research. If your skills in this regard are less well developed, however, do not fear. Quantitative political scientists are regularly criticised for trying to model and test anything and everything using advanced techniques, whether or not they are suitable for such advanced modelling and testing. Excellent quantitative dissertations can be produced that do not go beyond the use of tables, graphs, and basic techniques such as the calculation of percentages, ratios and averages. Moreover, should you feel confident, and where it is appropriate to do so, further light can be thrown on quantitative empirical issues through the calculation of standard deviations, through cross-tabulation and through the application of chi-square testing. All of these techniques can be self-taught and picked up fairly quickly from basic textbooks.

If you haven't studied quantitative techniques formally, however, the author would warn against trying to adopt more advanced methods in your dissertation. The basic problem is that the menu of available statistical tests is so extensive and many of these tests aim to do similar (but not the same) thing. In other words, unless you have either undergone the necessary formal training or unless your dissertation tutor is in a position to be able to give you a clear and unequivocal steer, avoid advanced statistical treatment of data. In this day and age the computer means that it is exceptionally easy to run hundreds of different tests on a set of data. Thus, this is one case where the proof of the pudding is not in the eating. Rather, the proof of the pudding is in the original selection from the available menu, i.e. it is not so much the process of *doing* the more complex tests that causes difficulties for the self-taught, but *the initial choice of which test to apply in which circumstances.*

Moreover, if you do need to develop your skills regarding the calculation of standard deviations or performing chi-square tests, for example, make sure that you learn how to work the tests by hand before leaping on to the computer. The best way of understanding exactly how any statistical procedure works (and by implication exactly what it can and cannot be used to achieve) is undoubtedly to practise the tests the old-fashioned, long-hand way. The author cannot really give better advice than this, writing as one who only just scraped through his compulsory class in statistics as an undergraduate. However, at a later date he started to take more interest in quantitative techniques, went back to the books, taught himself in much the way that has been described above and ended up producing a statistical doctorate. It can be done. The true danger lies in the simple observation that it can also be overdone – for instance, don't set out to determine the presence of heteroscedasity in a data set unless you know *exactly* what you are doing.

## DEDUCTION AND THE QUANTITATIVE DISSERTATION

In Chapter 2, brief descriptions of deduction and quantification were given and it was noted that there is something of a pattern of coexistence between the deductive way of thinking and the quantitative way of working. However, as also noted in Chapter 2, 'this is a relationship of association rather than one of necessity'. It is sensible to reiterate here that although not all quantitative work will be deductive in nature it is most commonly thus and, as a consequence, it is the deductive model of quantitative research that will be addressed in this chapter.

If you refer back to the plates at the beginning of the book you will see that deductive work starts off with a consideration of the theoretical. A deductive quantitative study may then start off from the theoretical premiss that there are ten different factors that influence voting behaviour (the ten different balls of wool in Plate 1). The task of the researcher would then be to check the result of feline frolics shown in Plate 2 – and its colour version on the website – to determine whether or not the theory has explanatory adequacy. In such an instance it will be no easy task to quantify that there are indeed ten different colours of wool, but it can be done. This is what the quantitative approach requires, enumerating the colours of wool present in the empirical world, guided by theory. If there are indeed ten colours of wool as predicted by the theory then the student would find it easy to concur with the theory. Similarly, if there are only nine colours present then the student may rightly be able to cast some doubt as to the explanatory adequacy of the theory when applied in an empirical context. The ease with which conclusions can be drawn is one of the significant advantages that deductive quantitative research has over inductive qualitative research. There either are ten colours of wool or there aren't, it isn't a matter for extended debate. As Roy Preece notes, 'One quality of deductive argument which makes it particularly attractive to scientists is that, if the argument is valid at all, then the conclusion is 100 per cent certain' (1994: 54).

You will also find that in a practical sense deductive quantitative work is structured differently from inductive qualitative work. In the deductive study you will spend time early in the dissertation process putting *order* into your work. That is, you will spend a good deal of time reading up on the relevant area of theory and logically operationalising this theory to ensure that you are intending to quantify the right things (namely that you are planning to count balls of wool rather than cats). You then have to consider how you will proceed to gather (and analyse) your data. If you were planning to do a quantitative study of balls of wool, for example, you would be advised to buy a magnifying glass in order to study Plate 2 at closer quarters. If, on the other hand, you were planning to do a quantitative dissertation on voting behaviour you might choose either to rely upon pre-existing data or to collect your own primary data. If you were to do the former you might, for example, choose to undertake a content analysis of recognised writings on the subject of voting behaviour with a view to determining congruence or lack of it within the literature for the ten key factors. In this example you would spend a good deal of time identifying the documentary sources that are to be analysed and producing a 'dictionary' of words associated with the ten key factors that you plan to search for in the documents. In the other example (collecting primary data) you may design a basic questionnaire, consisting of questions logically derived from the theoretical premiss that there are ten key factors that influence voting behaviour. In this instance you would also spend a considerable amount of time imposing order upon your study, but through the development of the questionnaire instead.

In the generally more inductive style of qualitative work, the researcher will usually spend less time sitting in the early stages of the process imposing order upon the dissertation study. In this model you gather your information at an earlier stage in the process and impose the order later on through data analysis. In other words, the quantitative dissertation tends to be character- ised by an extended period of planning in which order is imposed on the study followed by a period of data collection and analysis (that can actually be done quite quickly, at least when compared with the qualitative approach). More will be said about the qualitative approach in Chapter 6. In the meantime it is worth bearing in mind this practical distinction between the two different ways of working. Order is imposed on a quantitative study in the early stages of research and, as Bouma and Atkinson note (with particular relevance for the student undertaking a quantitative dissertation study):

> By now you should be well aware that doing research involves far more than data collection. The research process does not begin, nor does it end, with data collection. Before worthwhile data collection can be done the researcher must:
> 1 Focus the problem.
> 2 Identify and define the basic concepts involved.
> 3 Select variables that relate to each of the concepts under study.
> 4 Devise ways of measuring each of the variables.
> 5 Select a research design which will provide the desired information about the relation between variables.
> 6 Decide on a sampling procedure.
> 7 Draw the sample.
>
> Unless each of these essential first steps is completed, data

collection will often be done in a wasteful, haphazard, and unproductive way.

(Bouma and Atkinson 1995: 167)

To finish this section of the chapter the matter of drawing *deterministic* and *probabilistic* conclusions needs to be addressed. Students of politics, even if working in a deductive quantitative fashion, will almost certainly find that they are dealing (as is the case with the vast majority of instances in the social sciences) with quantification that is *probabilistic* in nature. To see the differences between the deterministic and the probabilistic refer to Table 5.1.

*Table 5.1* A comparison of probabilistic and deterministic conclusions

| Probabilistic conclusions | Deterministic conclusions |
| --- | --- |
| By studying a representative sample of the population of cigarette smokers we may draw the *probabilistic* conclusion that smoking twenty cigarettes a day means that you are *X per cent more likely* to develop lung cancer than a non-smoker | By studying a representative sample of the population of heroin users we may draw the *deterministic* conclusion that injecting X mg of the drug all at the same time *will definitely lead* to your death from overdose |

With reference to Table 5.1 do not worry if, after significant quantitative analysis, your dissertation's conclusions can only be presented in probabilistic terms. This is simply part and parcel of doing social scientific research and the study of politics is little different in this regard from the other social subjects. As Babbie notes below (and where the key probabilistic words in this quotation are 'tends to'):

> When we look for the causes of prejudice, we look for the reasons: the things that make some people prejudiced and others unprejudiced. Satisfactory reasons would include economic competition, religious ideology, political views, childhood experiences, amount and kind of education, and so forth. We know, for example, that education tends to reduce prejudice. That's the kind of causal explanation we accept as the end product of social research.
>
> (Babbie 1995: 65)

For further reading on the issues addressed in this section, please look to Babbie (1995) and Preece (1994). You could also do much worse than to look at Thomas Pettigrew's *How to Think Like a Social Scientist* (1996). If you haven't yet come across this little book in your academic career, you are hereby advised to purchase a copy – it will stand you in good stead.

## QUANTIFICATION

The quantitative tradition of research is, as noted in Chapter 2, a tradition, 'that encourages the dissertation student to make sense of their chosen political problem through the use of numbers, which are employed as either measures or indicators of relevant variables'. The numbers that will be generated for the purposes of data analysis are produced through the process of defining *quantifiable variables*. Thus, this section will be given over to considering the quantification of variables where, 'The idea of a variable is simple enough. A variable, as opposed to a constant, is anything, any attribute, that can vary in value; that is, take at least two values' (Ackroyd and Hughes 1992: 46). Ackroyd and Hughes, in common with many other commentators, describe the quantitative tradition as being about variable analysis, or, the disposition to see and describe social life as a collection of variables which, potentially, can be quantified and the relationships between them also measured and described in quantitative terms. These days it is not unreasonable to present variable analysis as a relatively coherent approach to social research, some would say *the* approach, which embraces not only the technical matters to do with data collection and analysis but also, importantly, a way of thinking about theoretical and empirical problems.

(Ackroyd and Hughes 1992: 42)

They continue:

The basic requirement of the approach is to think about concepts as empirical variables that can be measured through indices. This enables the data to be searched for patterns so placing theories within the constraints of empirical evidence. Indeed, it is through data collection and searching for patterns in those data that theory is elaborated.

(Ibid.: 45)

Thus, there is a need within a quantitative piece of research to identify the appropriate variables in the first instance (this will have been done as part of the operationalisation process) and to then attempt to quantify them. The manner in which quantification of variables is achieved will vary, depending upon the type of data with which one is working. There are four basic types of data that can be quantified in the social sciences (nominal, ordinal, interval and ratio) and three of them are likely to be of relevance to the student of politics (interval data is less likely to be significant than the other types).

1  *Nominal data* is information that is assigned a number where there is no clear reason for assigning that number as

opposed to any other. All that we are doing when we quantify nominal data is renaming a variable with a number (in much the same way that we could translate the variable's name into French or Arabic). For instance, consider data on gender. We could translate female into the number 1 and male into the number 2. We have then quantified the data, but only in a nominal sense, as there is no obvious reason for using these numbers for the male and female variables. We could just as easily translate female into the number 2 and male into the number 1. The only reason for nominal quantification is to allow us to perform statistical tests on pieces of information that do not have an obvious numerical value. Renaming the data with numbers means that these data can be subjected to simple (and mainly descriptive) statistical tests both within and across classes of variable. For example, we could calculate standard deviations for a consolidated set of exam marks and draw conclusions about the consistency of student performance by gender. A great deal of the quantitative data that we deal with in the social subjects is nominal. However, as the numbers are used simply to rename variables, we cannot perform arithmetic with them. It would be nonsense for example to try to divide female (1) by male (2). In this case $1 \div 2 \neq \frac{1}{2}$ because both the division and the result are meaningless in this context.

2 *Ordinal data* is a class of information which, while again not necessarily having an obvious numerical value, is at least ordered. Anyone who has ever filled in a questionnaire will be acquainted with this type of information e.g. more likely = 1, as likely = 2, less likely = 3 (note that by convention 'other' is usually given the value of 9). When quantifying ordinal data we need to ensure that we account for the natural order that exists within the information and that our approach is consistent. In other words, as long as we respect

that there is order in the data it does not matter whether 'more likely' is awarded the value of 1 or the value of 3. What does matter is that 'as likely' is awarded the value of 2. Again, we find that a good deal of the quantitative data that we deal with in the social subjects is ordinal in nature and that as with nominal data we are still unable to perform arithmetic with the numbers assigned to the variables e.g. 1 ('more likely) + 2 ("as likely") ≠ 3 ('less likely'). Another good example of ordinal data is social class – as, for instance, specified in Britain by classes I–V.

3 *Interval data* is of little relevance to the student of politics, but will be described for the sake of completeness. Basically, interval quantification can be accomplished when we know the size of the gap that exists between variables but are unable to determine a true zero point on the scale. Interval scales of data are then, similar to ordered scales, except we are able to define fairly accurately the size of the interval between variables. Intelligence quotients measured on a scale of 0–200 are an example of interval data. That is, we can be fairly confident that the intelligence gap between an IQ of 100 and an IQ of 80 is similar to that between an IQ of 100 and an IQ of 120. Nevertheless, the true position of the end points of the scale has never been accurately determined as nobody has an IQ of 0 and nobody has an IQ of 200. When working with interval data we can perform more advanced statistical tests and also addition and subtraction (although not multiplication or division as the position of the variables in relation to zero is not clear). For instance, consider the Celsius temperature scale, where we find that as a result of 0°C not being a true zero point 4°C − 2°C = 2°C but multiplication cannot be performed as 2°C × 2°C =550°C.

4 *Ratio data* is of great importance to many students of politics undertaking quantitative dissertations. Ratio data is that data

that usually has an obvious numerical value and can be quantified with reference to a true zero point. The unparalleled value of such data in quantitative analysis is that we can perform the full range of arithmetical, statistical and mathematical operations on it. The example most commonly given of ratio data in the literature is age. Age is measured against an accurate zero point (birth) and $25 \times 2 = 50$ and $50 \div 2 = 25$. You may have read elsewhere that there is very little use of ratio data in the social sciences. Be wary of this advice however. Whilst this may be sound advice for an anthropologist, the student of politics will find that: most demographic information is ratio data; most financial information is ratio data; most electoral information is ratio data; and that many performance indicators used by public authorities (across the whole range of governmental activity) utilise ratio data. Remember also that these are only illustrative examples and that there are others.

For further reading on quantification and variable analysis readers may not be surprised to note that the author highly recommends Ackroyd and Hughes (1992) to you – an excellent source.

## ASKING QUANTITATIVE RESEARCH QUESTIONS: FRAMING HYPOTHESES

As noted in Chapter 3, there are different ways in which research questions can be framed and the two main styles involve the writing either of hypotheses or of aims and objectives. It was also noted there that while either style can be employed in a quantitative study (or indeed in a qualitative one), the hypothesis construction is more commonly associated with the deductive quantitative study. Similarly, the aims and objectives construction is more commonly associated with inductive qualitative studies. As a consequence, hypotheses will be discussed in this chapter and aims and objectives in the next. Do remember, however, that *this does not mean* that quantitative studies must test hypotheses, nor does it mean that qualitative studies cannot make use of the hypothetical construction. Thus, should you wish to undertake a quantitative study that is based on aims and objectives rather than on a hypothesis, this will, in many instances, be perfectly acceptable and you will find the material on aims and objectives in the subsequent chapter on qualitative methods of relevance to yourself. As suggested in Chapter 3, if in doubt as to which means you use to frame your research question, ask your dissertation tutor for guidance. Their experience in supervising dissertations will allow them to make this judgement more easily than you can yourself. Before moving on to discuss hypotheses in detail, however, it is also worth bearing in mind the fact that the issue of whether you should choose to use a hypothesis or aims and objectives may not arise at all. That is, if your department has a preferred way of framing research questions, stick with it. There is little point in going against the grain, as, at the end of the day, there are few problems that cannot usefully be investigated from a starting point that involves the research question being stated in either form.

Regardless of the style in which a research question is asked, it serves one main role. The research question's role is to add focus and purpose to your study, consistent with the contents of your proposal's rationale. As Black has noted:

> Typically researchers would like to tackle significant problems and find meaningful answers. The most difficult part of starting a research project is often that of identifying the best question to ask, one that is meaningful, whose answer contributes to the discipline, and whose resulting research can be carried out within the resources available.
>
> (Black 1993: 24–25)

Thus, given that it has been established that there are two ways in which a meaningful research question can be framed in order to give shape to a good quality dissertation, the hypothesis will now be defined as follows:

A hypothesis is a provisional statement put forward for the sake of argument, or for the purpose of being tested. We have seen that one and the same statement can have a different status according to its place in a developing argument. A hypothesis is not an assertion since no truth is even claimed for it at first, and it certainly is not a conclusion although linguistically the form of words used could be exactly the same for an assertion, a hypothesis or a conclusion. It is important to have an open-minded attitude to a hypothesis; it is not a belief to be obstinately defended or selectively supported. It should certainly never be the aim of a research project to 'prove' that some pre-conceived notion is true . . .

(Preece 1994: 63)

In other words (at least as far as undertaking a dissertation with an empirical component is concerned), a hypothesis is simply a special type of sentence. In producing a hypothetical sentence the author will need to say something about what their theoretical underpinnings predict they ought to find and something about what they will investigate in the empirical world to enable the drawing of conclusions about the initial theory. With reference back to the plates, one might construct the hypothesis: 'When encountering ten balls of wool, feline theory predicts that a cat will steal one of the balls of wool and run away with it.' In this sentence one can see that a theoretical prediction is made and that reference has also been made to what will be investigated in the empirical world. In this particular instance of course, by studying Plate 2 and its coloured version on the website, we can see that the empirical findings lead us to reject the hypothesis. In this example, as long as our hypothesis was accurately and logically derived from feline theory, we can only conclude that feline theory may be flawed as the cat has not stolen a ball of wool and run away with it, but mixed up all ten colours instead. Remember, as noted in the above quotation from Preece (1994), it does not actually matter a great deal in terms of the value of our study if our hypothesis accurately predicted our findings. Regardless of the accuracy of the initial prediction, we have still been able to draw a meaningful conclusion that sheds some light on issues arising out of both the theoretical and the empirical worlds.

Hypotheses need not only be written as sentences, however. Natural scientists and economists regularly state their hypotheses mathematically. Although it would be less common to find a student of politics doing so, you can (if you really wish) state your hypotheses in this fashion also. For instance, hypotheses can be stated very precisely in algebraic terms:

- Revolutionary political action (x) is an emergent property of those sections of society which are poorly educated (y) and in material deprivation (z). This can be translated as, $x \neq y$, $x \neq z$, $y \neq z$, $x = y + z$;
- Willingness on the part of adults to engage in political protest (p), is closely related to educational attainment (e), can be translated as, $e \rightarrow p$.

Moreover, hypothetical sentences will also be written in a different fashion for the purely theoretical dissertation (although this will not be discussed in depth here). Look to the quotation below from Black in which different types of hypothesis are described.

1 Those that can be confirmed or refuted by direct

observation, assuming that the skill to make the appropriate observations exists . . .

2 Those that are confirmed or refuted by considering all possible negative alternatives. For example, all Britons are
Christians . . .

3 Those describing a central tendency involving traits of
groups. For example, the children in Blogg's School are of
average intelligence; workers performing under condition A
perform more efficiently than those under condition B.

(Black 1993: 30)

An example of the first category of hypothesis noted in the
quotation is the 'feline theory hypothesis' mentioned earlier and
the second category of hypothesis (the one that depends upon
mental processes only) is the type that would be employed in the
purely theoretical dissertation. It is the third type of hypothesis
that is most likely to be of relevance to the student of politics
engaged in deductive quantitative research.

Before such a hypothesis is framed, however, without a
shadow of doubt the student must ensure that they have understood their theoretical starting point and must ensure that their
operationalisation of the theory has been done in a manner that
is entirely logical. Otherwise there is a significant danger of
confusing the *independent* and the *dependent* variables when framing
the hypothesis. A confusion of this nature would fundamentally
undermine the academic merit of your dissertation and would
ruin your chances of gaining a good mark for your work. By way
of explanation of the distinction between independent and
dependent variables consider Black's statement:

Those variables that are suspected of affecting such events or
conditions, like heredity, nutrition, good books, are considered
*independent variables*. The resulting affected events are the
dependent variables since they are influenced by (depend on)

the other variables and not the other way round. For example, it might be possible that genetics affects intelligence, or even a propensity to crime, but becoming more intelligent or committing crimes will not change one's genetic make-up. Vitamins, or even baked beans, might help children to learn faster in the classroom, but learning faster in the classroom will have no effect on the quality of the vitamins or baked beans.

(Black 1993: 31)

Although the example relating to baked beans is clear for all to see, do not be lulled into a false sense of security, it is not always thus. For instance, consider the link between poverty and ill health. Does poverty cause ill health through inadequate housing, poor diet and stress or does ill health cause poverty through its effect upon employment prospects? Are both poverty and ill health actually a syndrome (i.e. where both are found together but are in fact caused by a common third factor)? To sum up then, Creswell notes that regardless of the type of hypothesis being framed, you should always try to do the following:

- *Develop the hypotheses, questions, or objectives from theory . . .*
- *Keep the independent and dependent variables separate and measure them separately . . .*
- *When writing this passage, select one form – write questions, objectives or hypotheses – but not a combination . . .*
- *If hypotheses are used, consider the alternative forms for writing them and make a choice on the audience for the research.*

(Creswell 1994: 73)

Creswell then proceeds to describe four types of hypothesis construction that can be usefully employed in social scientific research and gives examples of the types of wording which one might employ in each:

*Literary null hypothesis* (concept oriented, no direction):
There is no relationship between support services and academic persistence of nontraditional-aged college women.

*Literary alternative hypothesis* (concept oriented, directional):
The more that nontraditional-aged college women use support services the more they will persist academically.

*Operational null hypothesis* (operational, no direction):
There is no relationship between the number of hours non-traditional-aged women use the student union and their persistence at college after their freshman year.

*Operational alternative hypothesis* (operational, directional):
The more that nontraditional-aged women use the student union, the more they will persist at the college after their freshman year.

(Ibid.: 74)

The style of hypothesis that you write for your dissertation will essentially depend on three things, the nature of your problem, your own personal preference and, of course, the advice of your dissertation tutor. However, where you plan to undertake certain types of statistical testing (e.g. chi-square testing), you will find that it is necessary to set down a null hypothesis if you are going to be able to analyse your data properly at a later stage. As can be seen from the Creswell examples of null hypotheses though, all that the writing of a null hypothesis really involves is the prediction of there being no relationship between variables rather than a prediction of there being one. Although this may seem like a minor semantic difference it is actually important to think about what tests you will want to perform on your quantitative data at the hypothesis-framing stage as this will determine the type of wording that is adopted. As Black notes:

There is no necessity for all hypotheses to be stated as null hypotheses, but if the intent is to make inferences to a larger population through a study that collects data to be processed statistically, then a null hypothesis is in order. While a general hypothesis may propose a cause and effect relationship, a null hypothesis should not, since all that the resulting statistical tests will be able to determine will be whether or not the relationship occurred by chance or not.

(Black 1993: 35)

Finally, to conclude this section of the chapter, please bear in mind that you *can* undertake quantitative research based on aims and objectives as opposed to hypotheses and that you should speak to your dissertation tutor about how you are proposing to frame your research question. It is essential that both the type of research question adopted and the wording of it be agreed. As previously noted, an error in the research question can fundamentally undermine the academic merit of your dissertation. Further reading on hypotheses (and indeed aims and objectives) can be found in: Babbie (1995); Black (1993); Bouma and Atkinson (1995); Creswell (1993); McNeill (1990); Preece (1994).

## METHODS FOR PRIMARY QUANTITATIVE RESEARCH

If you are planning to do a quantitative piece of research for your dissertation and need to gather your own primary information, you may already be aware that there are two main branches of the quantitative tradition that are employed when investigating the subject matter of the social sciences. These two branches are respectively the survey method and the experimental method, although this section of the chapter will dwell only briefly on the former (the issues have been expounded at great length elsewhere by many other authors) and will only really mention the latter. Experimentation in the social sciences is in large part similar to experimentation in the natural sciences and is mainly used in the study of psychology. Although there are instances of experimental research being used to investigate some of the problems of economics and also some decision-making processes, there is unlikely to be much mileage for the average student of politics in adopting the experimental method. Consider the following definition:

> A *survey* design provides a quantitative or numeric description of some fraction of the population – the sample – through the data collection process of asking questions of people ... This data collection, in turn, enables a researcher to generalise their findings from a sample of responses to a population. An *experiment* tests cause-and-effect relationships in which the researcher randomly assigns subjects to groups. The researcher manipulates one or more independent variables and determines whether these manipulations cause an outcome ... The researcher tests cause and effect because, theoretically, all (or most) variables between the manipulated variable and the outcome are controlled in the experiment.
>
> (Creswell 1994: 117)

In reading this quotation you may recall from Chapter 2 that most political problems are deeply embedded within a social and historical context (i.e. are culturally and temporally bound). Thus, such problems are not particularly amenable to investigation through experimentation. For example, it would be neither practical nor ethically appropriate for us to create government departments or problem housing estates just so that we could carry out experiments on them by manipulating variables. Indeed, even in those social scientific sub-fields where the experimental method is more commonly used, we must seek to remind ourselves that the effect on human behaviour of being involved in an experiment can be quite dramatic and can seriously affect the validity of findings (commonly termed the Hawthorne effect). Unlike molecules, humans generally volunteer (often in return for payment) to take part in social scientific experiments and are only too aware of what is going on. Moreover, where findings have been generated in a strictly controlled setting, it is often difficult to assess the extent to which we can then accurately extrapolate from these findings to say anything meaningful about their meaning in an everyday empirical social setting. In an experiment the application of specific stimuli to the experimental group is carefully controlled but it is difficult to assess what the true effect would be of applying the same stimuli in an ordinary social setting where they will get mixed with other (often competing) stimuli. The empirical social world is, after all, a bit like Plate 2.

Should you, however, be contemplating undertaking an experiment as part and parcel of a very specialised dissertation in politics, please refer to Ackroyd and Hughes (1992) and Babbie (1995) for further information on how to proceed.

But there is greater scope for the application of survey methods in addressing political problems. Although there is some disagreement over what the word 'survey' does and does not mean, it will be used in this book to describe structured and semi-structured interviews and questionnaires. In designing a piece of survey research, with reference back to Chapter 2, assuming that your operationalisation has been logical and that you've followed a recognised method, your study ought to have been imbued with construct validity and reliability respectively. With reference back to Chapter 3, assuming that you have undertaken a thorough review of the relevant literature, your study ought to have been imbued with content validity. Thus, in designing the survey itself we have to ensure that we abide by the principles of ethical conduct outlined in Chapter 2 and that we build representativeness into the study through our sampling. As Ragin has noted:

> The starting point of quantitative analysis is the idea that the best route to understanding basic patterns and relationships is to examine patterns across many cases ... Images that are constructed from broad patterns of covariation are considered general because they condense evidence on many cases. The greater the number of cases, the more general the pattern.
>
> (Ragin 1994: 131)

## SURVEYS

Ragin's sentiments can be expressed in a more straightforward way however. Catherine Hakim notes, 'If surveys offer the bird's eye view, qualitative research offers the worm's eye view' (Hakim 2000: 36). This is an excellent analogy. If one considers the bird soaring high, it is somewhat detached from the world it is looking down on and takes in a big-picture view. It is able to see the landscape as a whole and can see all of the variables that make up that landscape at the same time. It cannot however necessarily always see the detailed nature of interactions between these variables. Thus, as mentioned in Chapter 2, the quantitative survey approach is representative, but owing to the distance from which the world is viewed cannot always provide much in the way of comment on the detailed nature of inter-actions – leading to criticisms over validity. The worm on the other hand is making observations close up to the world it is living in but does not necessarily know what lies behind the next stone, let alone have a clear idea about the role of that stone in the wider world. Owing to its detailed view however, it is more likely than the bird to spot exactly how certain small-scale interactions actually occur. Thus, from Chapter 2, the qualitative tradition lacks representativeness. Owing to the distance from which the world is viewed though, qualitative means of investigation can provide a more detailed and often more valid commentary as to how certain interactions occur (although it cannot be assumed that these comments have value beyond the small part of the world that has been viewed).

In terms of reliability, surveys again score highly when compared to more qualitative means of investigation. As Hakim notes:

> One of the main attractions of the sample survey design (both for policy research and theoretical research) is its *transparency* or *accountability* – the fact that the methods and procedures used can be made visible and accessible to other parties . . . so that the implementation, as well as the overall research design, can be assessed. In contrast, many of the methods used by other research designs remain hidden, or not easily accessible. (For example, readers of research reports cannot readily have access to the tape recordings of depth interviews, to a case study database, or to the administrative records used for a study.)
>
> (Hakim 2000: 77)

Thus, the survey method is more reliable and representative than its qualitative cousins, but cannot always provide the same degree of validity in its conclusions, owing to the fact that the focus is on investigating a comparably bigger picture, but in less depth. As noted above, in this book the term 'survey' is used as an umbrella description covering all types of structured and semi-structured interview and questionnaire. As Ackroyd and Hughes have noted, there will be few readers of this book who are not already acquainted with these techniques for gathering primary data, although this acquaintance may in some instances be a fairly superficial one:

Most of us living in industrialised countries are familiar with social surveys of one type or another. Few of us would be surprised to find an interviewer on our doorstep asking us to give a few moments of our time 'to answer one or two questions' on our voting habits, which TV programmes we watch or which washing powder we use. Some of us may have taken part in an academic survey; most of us will have taken part in the census. Week by week we read of the latest opinion polls on this or that. Accordingly, while most of us may not be *au fait* with the technicalities of surveys, we are likely to have an intuitive grasp of what surveys are about; they are concerned with finding out how many people, within a defined social-cum-geographical area, hold particular views or opinions about things, events or individuals, do particular activities; possess particular qualities; and so on.

(Ackroyd and Hughes 1992: 65)

A number of systems for classifying surveys exist. For example, Ackroyd and Hughes (1992) distinguish between factual, attitude, social psychological and explanatory surveys. Hakim (2000) also distinguishes between different survey types, which she terms ad hoc sample surveys, regular surveys and longitudinal studies. For readers interested in these distinctions, you are referred to these sources. However, it is most likely that the student of politics who is to carry out a survey as a means of gathering primary data for their dissertation will be engaged in carrying out the type of survey described by Hakim as an ad hoc sample survey. She notes:

The ad hoc sample survey offers a multi-purpose research design with many advantages for both policy research and theoretical research. The application of sampling allows the production of descriptive statistics that are representative (on a national, regional or state basis) of the whole study population but at much lower cost than with a census of every member of the whole study population in question. Sample surveys also allow associations between factors mapped and measured. For example, they can show not only what proportions of working men and women are in professional occupations, but also what proportions of those in professional occupations have appropriate qualifications and what proportions of those holding such qualifications also hold professional jobs. Even without going into causal analysis to ascertain the reasons for such relationships, the bare fact of such associations, whether strong or weak, can be useful information. Thirdly, sample survey designs can be used to study causal processes, to develop and test explanations for particular associations or social patterns. This use of the survey has been facilitated and extended by the development of complex and sophisticated analysis techniques that are readily available in packages such as SPSS.

(Hakim 2000: 76)

Within the above definition of the ad hoc sample survey technique it is possible to fit both structured and semi-structured survey techniques, but not unstructured ones (this latter group of techniques will be discussed in Chapter 6). By structured and semi-structured techniques the author means structured and semi-structured interviews (whether conducted face to face or by telephone) and structured and semi-structured questionnaires (whether distributed and returned by hand, by post or by electronic means). There are very close similarities in the design of the tools of the quantitative survey that will be discussed presently. Bear in mind once more of course that there is not the space in this book to go into detailed extended discussion of these matters. Where the reader feels that they would like to have more information on this or on that, please look to the further reading that is recommended at the end of this section of the chapter.

Ackroyd and Hughes make the distinction between the structured and semi-structured techniques in discussing face-to-face interviews, but their words are equally applicable to the design of telephone interviews, postal questionnaires, etc. They define the structured interview as being one where:

> The same questions and the order in which they appear on the schedule would be administered, in a survey, to all respondents by all interviewers in the same way: this is to standardise stimuli. That is, in an effort to ensure that any variations in replies respondents provide are not artifacts of variations in the way in which the questions were asked, each respondent should be given the same questions in the same serial order.
>
> (Ackroyd and Hughes 1992: 103)

By contrast, they define the semi-structured interview as being one where:

> The relative weight of standardised and non-standardised items can vary from research to research. The most common arrangement is to use the standardised format for 'face-sheet' information, such as age, sex, marital status, educational experience and other relevant data of a demographic character. The less standardised section is used to elicit information more varied and qualitative in character.
>
> (Ibid: 104)

The real key to designing a quantitative data gathering tool though, especially if semi-structured, is to pointedly avoid including too many open-ended questions. If, in developing such a tool you find that you need to ask a great many open-ended questions, you may need to re-think your data collection altogether. Do you really need all of the qualitative information that you're going to collect through the open-ended responses? If you don't really need them all, cut back on the number of open-ended questions. If you don't there is every chance that you will come to regret having asked them when the time for data analysis comes. On the other hand, if you do need all of the qualitative data, perhaps you should in fact be undertaking a qualitative dissertation and not a quantitative one at all. There are a great many sources available to you that will give greater detail on the development of questionnaires and interview schedules. However, in brief, you could do worse than to take the advice of Earl Babbie. He has suggested that whenever we are engaged in the design of quantitative research tools we need to ensure that we've addressed the following points:

- the balance that exists between open-ended and closed-ended questions (as already discussed above);
- the clarity of questions;
- Avoiding double-barrelled questions (i.e. a question should not ask for respondents to comment on two or more variables with only one response);
- that all questions will be ones which the respondents are competent to answer;
- that all of the questions are entirely relevant to our research purpose (they should be if your operationalisation has been logical);
- that all the questions are relatively short and unbiased; and
- that questions are not posed in a negative way (i.e. ask 'do you agree with the following' rather than 'do you not agree with the following').

(Babbie 1995: 142–7)

In general, the author concurs with Babbie's advice. There can, however, be dangers associated with asking questions that are too short as well as ones that are too long. As a sentence grows in length, this is sometimes a result of increased focus and accuracy rather than a result of verbosity. You may find for example that when using the grammar facility on a computer to check your academic writing it sometimes accuses you of writing long sentences that cannot be easily broken down further. This is because in academic writing there is sometimes no obvious way of cutting sub-clauses (that are included for the purposes of clarity and accuracy) out of a sentence without detracting from its precision.

Once you have developed your questionnaire or interview schedule it is always wise to subject it to piloting. This will help you to ensure that the questions are suitably clear and that the respondents are indeed competent to answer them. If clarity or competence issues raise their head you need to do something about them if you are to protect the validity, the reliability and in some cases even the representativeness of your work. Finally, as discussed more fully in Chapter 2, when developing quantitative survey tools, bear in mind the benefits associated with using standardised question formats that have already been tried and tested.

In administering your structured or semi-structured questionnaires or interviews there are of course a range of means available to you, as has already been noted. Chief amongst these is the face-to-face method, where you either conduct an interview in person or hand somebody a questionnaire, they fill it in and you collect it back from them. The telephone interview is also a means by which primary quantitative data can be gathered, as is the questionnaire distributed by some other means (e.g. through the postal service or by electronic means). There are of course advantages and disadvantages associated with each means of gathering your primary quantitative data regarding both maximising the effort expended by yourself and maximising response rates with a view to ensuring representativeness. For instance, Babbie notes that:

A properly designed and executed interview survey ought to achieve a completion rate of at least 80 to 85 percent ... Respondents seem more reluctant to turn down an interviewer standing on their doorstep than they are to throw away a mail questionnaire.

(Babbie 1995: 264)

You will then have to exercise your own judgement regarding means of distribution. See Table 5.2 for a brief synopsis of the tensions that exist between effort expended and response rates. As ever, if you're in need of further advice on means of distribution, ask your dissertation tutor.

*Table 5.2* The trade-off between effort expended and response rates

| Means of data gathering | Effort required | Response rates |
|---|---|---|
| Face to face | Great | High |
| Telephone | Medium | Medium |
| Postal, electronic, etc. | Small | Low |

To conclude this section of the chapter, bear in mind that what has been offered here is only a very cursory review of the issues associated with gathering primary data using survey methods. For further information on the detail of developing and administering structured and semi-structured questionnaires and interviews, please refer to any of: Ackroyd and Hughes (1992); Allan and Skinner (1991); Babbie (1995); Bell (1999); Blaxter *et al.* (1996); Bouma and Atkinson (1995); Creswell (1994); Evans (1984); Gill and Johnson (1991); Hakim (2000); May (1997); Moser and Kalton (1971); Preece (1994); Saunders, *et al.* (1997); de Vaus (1996).

## ANALYSING SECONDARY DATA SOURCES

Although a small number of departments may *require* students to do their own data collection as part and parcel of the dissertation process, most are happy to allow students to undertake dissertations that draw upon secondary data (i.e. data that has been collected by someone other than yourself). There is a rich array of quantitative secondary data available to the student of politics, much of it collected by governmental organisations, but not only by them. Political parties, voluntary bodies, private companies and the media are all sources of data that can prove useful to the student of politics. Last but not least of course, you will find that your institution's library is packed with data that has arisen out of academic research. Each and every scholarly journal will contain a number of articles, most of which report and comment upon the findings of a programme of research. Overall, there is no end of secondary data available for you to draw upon in researching and writing a dissertation, data that can be sourced through using the types of literature searching technique that were discussed in the last chapter. Moreover, please note that a stronger emphasis is placed upon primary data collection in some of the other social sciences. Thus, while you may read elsewhere that you have to gather your own primary data in order to do a dissertation, do not accept that things are necessarily thus. As ever, if unsure whether you are expected to collect your own primary data or not, ask your dissertation tutor for advice. If they say that you must, then you do it. On the other hand, if they say that you need not you're in a privileged position. You can then decide whether or not there's likely to be suitable secondary data upon which you can draw, in order to save yourself the time and effort that is required in collecting your own. Indeed, if you can find robust, relevant secondary data sources from which you can draw, you may well end up working with a larger and better quality data set than you would have been able to collect yourself. Think for example about demographic data – why collect your own? The government collects it for you (in the United Kingdom at least), working with massive samples on an annual basis and conducting a census of the entire population of approximately 60 million once a decade. Data simply does not come much better than this. Naturally, secondary data sources are not confined to demography and, if you look to the academic journals, you will find that there will already be pre-existing data sets for many or most political problems that are amenable to quantification.

Do not, however, be tempted to treat secondary data as some form of panacea. Remember, political parties, private companies and voluntary organisations generally collect and make available sets of data because they wish to add supporting evidence to some particular point that they're keen to make. As a student of politics you should be more aware of this than anyone else. You will therefore need to make a judgement on whether such data sets have been generated in a manner that is valid, reliable and representative. For instance, on 9 November 1997 *The People* (a British tabloid Sunday newspaper) covered nearly all of its front page with a 'WORLD EXCLUSIVE' banner headline that reads as follows: 'Sensational result of *People* poll . . . DIANA *WAS* MURDERED! 98% believe plot killed Di and Dodi'. However, when one looks more carefully at the article about the late Princess of Wales, one discovers that what has actually happened is that 5,600 people (from a UK population of about 60 million) have self-selected themselves to telephone a tabloid newspaper poll and record their opinion on a conspiracy theory. Revealingly, within the accompanying article *The People* clearly refers to its role in trying to investigate alternative explanations for the death of the couple concerned. Thus, the paper had put to its readers a particular account of events and then sought to get them to add quantitative evidence to support the point that they'd been trying to make. Not only is this a somewhat tautological process, but we were not told how many readers of *The People* did not trouble themselves to telephone in with their answer to the question 'Were Diana and Dodi killed as part of a secret operation?' As *The People* is an established national newspaper, the author can only guess that the rate of non-response must be many times higher than the rate of response. This is not the sort of secondary source upon which one would want to rely in producing a dissertation. Indeed, the only conclusion that can safely be drawn from instances such as this is that the production of a set of figures does not in itself imply that these figures have been produced with due regard for academic rigour.

A second problem that can be faced by those drawing upon secondary sources of data is that as most political problems are culturally and temporally bound this does tend to limit the extent to which you can usefully apply much of the information that you come across. For example, the year in which this book is published, 2001, sees the ten-yearly census being conducted in the United Kingdom. As a consequence of this, any person wishing to use British census data in 2000, say, is disadvantaged in comparison with someone who had been able to use the census data of 1991 in 1993. That does not mean that secondary data taken from older or overseas sources is entirely worthless – just that you may need to complement the secondary data by conducting your own data gathering exercise to overcome the issue of the secondary material being either culturally or temporally bound. Indeed, there is often merit in your faithfully repeating a study from another country or from another period in time to determine through comparison the extent to which a given problem is in fact bound by culture or time. (Please note that the comparative method will be addressed directly in Chapter 7 when discussing the theoretical dissertation. It can, however, also be usefully employed when addressing political problems that have an empirical component.)

As far as suggesting precisely which sources of secondary data will be of particular use to you, the author is not really in a position to comment on countries other than the United Kingdom. That said, similar information does tend to be available in most developed countries and one of the central roles of international organisations (e.g. UN agencies, the European Union, OECD, etc.) is the collation, comparison and distribution of comparative data. Now that so much of this data is to be found available in an electronic format, accessible from wherever you are in the world, this can make the task of finding good secondary data sets with which to work much easier.

To return to the data which you may find available in your country of study, however, the author has put together a very brief summary of the sources of information which may prove to be of use to the student based in the United Kingdom. It is likely, as already noted, that similar information can be found in most other parts of the developed world. Over and above the census, Hakim refers to a range of surveys that are carried out by the British Government on a regular basis and these include the following:

- Family Expenditure Survey
- Family Resources Survey
- General Household Survey
- Health Survey
- Housing Survey
- International Passenger Survey
- Labour Force Survey
- National Travel Survey

(Hakim 2000: 99)

All the data collected in these surveys is put into the public domain after analysis and there are many more examples of data available to the public that has been collected and published by governmental organisation in the United Kingdom. For instance, the British government publishes annual league tables of examination results and other indicators for all schools in the country (i.e. for both state and fee-paying schools); it also publishes annually sets of indicators to indicate the extent to which the UK is moving towards a path of sustainable development. All local authorities in the United Kingdom are obliged to publish baseline data relating to economy and efficiency across all areas of service provision, etc.

In terms of accessing data sets generated by academics, there are of course, many relevant journals, packed with research findings. Over and above this as far as secondary quantitative data are concerned, we in the United Kingdom are blessed with the existence of *The Data Archive*, housed at the University of Essex, which now contains nearly 10,000 sets of social scientific data which can be accessed electronically. The Archive's website (<http://www.data-archive.ac.uk/>) contains links to other similar sites overseas and is the best place to find out more about this resource. If you wish to use materials from the Archive you are advised to speak to your dissertation tutor and get them to help you (be warned as well that some data sets are subject to restrictions on access).

Finally, to conclude this section on the use of secondary sources the role of content analysis must be mentioned. You may have encountered this technique of quantitative documentary analysis during your studies. It is undoubtedly a method that has grown in popularity with the advent of a variety of powerful computer programmes that take the pain out of analysing the contents of documents in a quantitative fashion. Nevertheless, content analysis remains to an extent a controversial technique, the butt of many a joke about counting words. Do not be deceived by such derision, however. Admittedly, the counting of words is central to the process of content analysis, but this does not mean that this is all that there is to it, far from it. No matter what your views on content analysis are, it is a fairly specialised technique and one that is more likely to be employed by a student of information science than a student of politics as part of an undergraduate dissertation (although it would not be at all surprising to find postgraduate students of politics employing such techniques). However, should you already be acquainted with content analysis, be interested in using it and have both the necessary software and specialist supervision arrangements available to you, by all means use it as a basis for a quantitative political dissertation. With the right conditions, you may find that you are able to produce a high quality and original undergraduate dissertation. See Weber (1990) for information on the technique. If all of the four conditions noted above are not present however, give it a miss as the basis of a dissertation. You can learn how to do it some other time.

For further reading on working with secondary sources of data, refer to: Hakim (2000); May (1997); Saunders *et al.* (1997).

## SUMMARY

From this, we may conclude:

1  that a quantitative dissertation in politics can be produced without special mathematical ability on the student's part;
2  that the *order* tends to be imposed upon a piece of quantitative work in the early stages of the study;
3  that the quantitative political dissertation is likely to draw probabilistic conclusions;
4  that the student of politics is likely to work with three types of quantitative data (nominal, ordinal and ratio);
5  that quantitative work can be based on either a hypothesis or aims and objectives but that the former is more commonly used;

6 that the student of politics is unlikely to be involved in experimental research;

7 that survey techniques may prove valuable to the student of politics in gathering primary data;

8 that such survey techniques can, however, have weaknesses, especially regarding the drawing of conclusions about the detailed nature of mechanisms underlying interactions between variables;

9 that a wide range of secondary sources are available to the student of politics who is engaged in researching and writing a dissertation; and

10 that, just because quantitative studies are based on numbers, this doesn't necessarily mean that they are more accurate than other types of study (e.g. the example of the late Princess of Wales on pp. 119–20).

## TEST YOUR KNOWLEDGE OF THIS CHAPTER

Please refer to p. 19 for details.

# 6

## INDUCTION, QUALIFICATION AND THE EMPIRICAL DISSERTATION

### Understanding feline fun

## INTRODUCTION

If you have just finished reading Chapter 5, do not worry – this one will be shorter. Had qualitative methods been discussed first, then this would have become the larger chapter, as there is a need in any book like this to distinguish between the two basic approaches of doing research for a dissertation that addresses both theoretical and empirical issues. Consequently, this chapter can begin with most of the task of drawing distinctions between the quantitative and qualitative traditions already completed through Chapters 2 and 5. By default then, this is a shorter chapter, but that is not to intimate that there is less to be said about the qualitative tradition. As noted in Chapter 2, the qualitative tradition has an especially important role to play in political research and it is fully the author's intention to do it justice here.

The qualitative tradition in the social sciences is a long one. Think back to the discussion of the work of Max Weber in Chapters 1 and 2 (and it can be traced back still further). Following the Second World War, however, the qualitative approach lost some of its potency and there was a concerted attempt by many political scientists (and social scientists working in most other fields) to drive their subjects down a more quantitative road. Remember the note in Chapter 5 to the effect that, 'Quantitative political scientists are regularly criticised for trying to model and test anything and everything using advanced techniques, whether or not they are suitable for such advanced modelling and testing.' This criticism has come about in large part as a backlash against taking quantification too far in the post-War era. As noted in Chapter 5, some political matters are undoubtedly suited to quantitative analysis, e.g. electoral data come ready-quantified. Others, however, are less well suited. For instance, it would not appear to be sensible to investigate the legislative impact of a Parliamentary term simply by reference to the number of laws passed. It is for instance very easy to pass large quantities of legislation that involve marginal change to obscure areas of law that will have only a minimal impact upon the life and business of the country. Such legislative change would be unlikely to cause extended Parliamentary debate, and, as a consequence, lots of it could be passed in the time available. Interestingly, it was at about the same time as computerised analysis of findings started to allow for very sophisticated and advanced quantitative analysis (1960s and 1970s) that the qualitative resurgence was witnessed. As noted by Blaxter et al., 'Qualitative research has become increasingly popular over the last two decades' (Blaxter et al. 1996: 61). Thus, the qualitative methods of social scientific research are once again widely employed by scholars across the range of social subjects, politics included.

Of course, as noted in Chapter 2, qualitative research tends to be both unrepresentative and heavily dependent on personal interpretation. Consequently, the qualitative tradition is sometimes lambasted as a poor man's method, unscientific and lacking in rigour. Admittedly, one of the difficulties encountered by those engaged in qualitative research is that, 'Unlike with quantitative designs, few writers agree on a precise procedure for data collection, analysis, and reporting of qualitative research' (Creswell 1994: 143). However, as was also noted in Chapters 2 and 5, the quantitative method displays a range of weaknesses of its own. Remember that it has been one of the themes of this book (along with many others) to suggest that methods of research should be suited to the problem in hand. If this is so, in considering that the qualitative tradition attempts to attribute meaning to the ongoings of the empirical world through the interpretation of them, you will almost certainly recognise that qualitative methods have a role to play in the investigation of political problems.

## INDUCTION AND THE QUALITATIVE DISSERTATION

In Chapter 2, brief descriptions of induction and qualification were given and it was noted that there is something of a pattern of coexistence between the inductive way of thinking and the qualitative way of working. However, as also noted in Chapter 2, 'this is a relationship of association rather than one of necessity'. It is sensible to reiterate here that although not all qualitative work will be inductive in nature the vast bulk of it is and, as a consequence, it is the inductive model of qualitative research that will be addressed in this chapter.

If you refer back to the plates at the start of the book you will see that inductive work starts with an investigation of the empirical. An inductive qualitative study will then start off with an investigation of the results of feline fun shown in Plate 2 (i.e. the empirical). The end result of the study would hopefully be the construction or modification of some theoretical explanation for this feline fun (as represented by the ten different balls of wool in Plate 3). In such an instance it will be no easy task to establish the motivations of the cat in messing up all the balls of wool but this is what the qualitative approach seeks to do, through a 'deep' investigation focused upon a small part of the world. Thus, the drawing of conclusions is, in comparison with the quantitative tradition, fraught with difficulties. It cannot be denied that this is a process that depends in large part upon the researcher's interpretation of data drawn from an unrepresentative sample using unreliable methods. As such, bearing in mind the words of Creswell (1994) in the quotation above, it is often easier for the critic to snipe at the findings of qualitative research than at the findings of quantitative work (assuming that recognised quantitative procedures have been followed).

In comparison with quantitative research, qualitative investigations have been characterised as being, 'relatively unstructured' (Bouma and Atkinson 1995: 205). This statement reflects the fact that whereas order in a quantitative study is imposed in the study's early stages, as noted in Chapter 5, 'In the generally more inductive style of qualitative work, the researcher will usually spend less time sitting in the early stages of the process imposing order upon the dissertation study. In this model you gather your information at an earlier stage in the process and impose the order later on through data analysis.' In other words, the qualitative dissertation tends to be characterised by a shorter period of initial planning than the quantitative, followed by a period of data collection and an extended period of data analysis in which order is imposed on the study. With reference back to the plates, you can imagine that the task of imposing order on Plate 2 is a slow, laborious and sometimes painful task.

Because the empirical world is investigated at an early stage in the qualitative study, the theoretical conclusions of the process are often referred to as 'grounded theories' (the word 'grounded' being a reference to their being grounded in the empirical). Although deductive thinkers such as Popper (1980) have argued that it doesn't actually matter where theories come from, many proponents of modern qualitative research would argue vehemently that it does. There is, they would argue, surely more explanatory merit in a theory that has been built on investigation of the empirical world that surrounds us than in a theory that has been concocted in the minds of people who haven't troubled themselves to take a careful look at the world around them first. One of those who makes this argument most clearly (and was involved in the revival of the qualitative approach in the social sciences from the 1960s onwards) is Anselm Strauss. In his many writings he has argued convincingly about the merits of the inductive qualitative study and if further information about the fundamental basis of this approach is needed, just about any source you come across that includes his name as an author will be of use to you. He notes the following:

> What is a grounded theory? A *grounded theory* is one that is inductively derived from the study of the phenomenon it represents. That is, it is discovered, developed, and provisionally verified through systematic data collection and analysis of data pertaining to that phenomenon. Therefore, data collection, analysis, and theory stand in reciprocal relationship with each other. One does not begin with a theory, then prove it. Rather, one begins with an area of study and what is relevant to that area is allowed to emerge.
>
> (Strauss and Corbin 1990: 23)

Therefore, to sum up this section, the main purpose of an inductive qualitative study is to draw conclusions from an investigation of the empirical world that will assist either in the development of new theory that is 'grounded' in the empirical or in the modification of existing theories in light of empirical findings.

Note, though, that even arch-proponents of the qualitative method do acknowledge that the choice of method should always be determined in the first instance by:

> the nature of the research problem. Some areas of study naturally lend themselves more to qualitative types of research ... Qualitative methods can be used to uncover and understand what lies behind any phenomenon about which little is known. It can be used to gain novel and fresh slants on things about which quite a bit is already known. Also, qualitative methods can give the intricate details of phenomena that are difficult to convey with quantitative methods.
>
> (Strauss and Corbin 1990: 19)

Moreover, despite the fact that there are undoubtedly many benefits to be derived from conducting a qualitative piece of research for your dissertation in politics, you must at all times remember that the qualitative approach to research, like the quantitative, has specific strengths and weaknesses (as previously discussed in Chapter 2). The qualitative tradition then, while it does not necessarily have more problems associated with it than the quantitative, certainly has *different* problems associated with it. Bearing in mind that the quantitative methods of research can sometimes prove weak when it comes to providing us with validity when explaining the detailed nature of interactions, Hakim notes that conversely:

> The great strength of qualitative research is the *validity* of the data obtained ... Its main weakness is that small numbers of respondents cannot be taken as representative, even if great

care is taken to choose a fair cross-section of the type of people who are the subjects of the study.

(Hakim 2000: 36)

## INTERPRETATION

As noted in the quotation from Creswell (1994) earlier in this chapter, there is less agreement in the literature as to exactly how qualitative procedures for data collection and analysis should be carried out. To some extent this simply comes with the territory – qualitative work is far more personal in style than quantitative work and one consequence of this is that the ways in which things are done depend more upon personal preference. However, although there are no books available on qualitative techniques that tell you exactly what to do, how to do it and in what order in the same way as there are about quantitative techniques, there is a general agreement in the literature that qualitative research is:

> concerned with collecting and analysing information in as many forms, chiefly non-numeric, as possible. It tends to focus on exploring, in as much detail as possible, smaller numbers of instances or examples which are seen as being interesting or illuminating, and aims to achieve 'depth' rather than 'breadth'.
>
> (Blaxter *et al.* 1996: 60)

This is consistent with Hakim's assertion, already quoted in Chapter 5 that, 'If surveys offer the bird's eye view, qualitative research offers the worm's eye view' (2000: 36). As noted in Chapter 5 also, the worm can only investigate things up close and does not necessarily know much about the wider world. Consequently, while it can only investigate a very small part of the world, it can do so in great detail. This is the crux of the qualitative tradition of social scientific research –

unrepresentative yet valid. However, as noted in Chapters 2 and 5 there are also reliability issues connected with qualitative research. These issues arise from its interpretive nature. By way of contrast, readers will recall that in Chapter 5 there was a note made to the effect that, 'There is often merit in your faithfully repeating a study from another country or from another period in time to determine through comparison the extent to which a given problem is in fact bound by culture or time.' Such an approach is possible with a quantitative procedure as it is possible to replicate (to a considerable extent at least) the methods of others. In other words, a questionnaire or interview schedule can be reused, the data collected can be analysed using the same statistical procedures, etc. However, as Creswell notes, 'Qualitative research is interpretative research. As such, the biases, values and judgements of the researcher become stated explicitly in the research project. Such openness is considered to be useful and positive' (Creswell 1994: 7). It may therefore be inherently less easily reproduced on subsequent occasions.

Thus, while the interpretation which the qualitative researcher brings to the process of 'sampling' (or perhaps the term 'identification' is more appropriate) of instances for study, to the collection of data, and to the analysis of findings is integral to 'deep' investigation of a very small part of the world, this dependence renders the approach less than reliable. Interpretation cannot be repeated. It is largely guided by value systems and, even where two people share a set of basic values, they may still interpret the empirical world in a different fashion. As students of politics you should be more aware of this than others. For instance, is it possible for two people coming from different ideological stances to interpret data in the same way? While the classical liberal might see the state's imposition of a minimum wage as an attack on freedom the social democrat might see it as a means of ensuring freedom for the less well-off in society. (See

Kuhn (1970) for further information on this point.) Both camps would be able to produce data to support their position. Moreover, as noted above, even where people share a set of basic values it does not mean that they will interpret the empirical world in the same light. Consider the example of Cabinet Government – all members of the Cabinet will have at least broad agreement in terms of basic political values, otherwise they would not all be in the same party, tied to the same manifesto promises. However, when it comes to the detailed nature of prioritising the problems of the empirical world that surrounds them, arguments start. Interpretive methods then, are unreliable. For further reading on interpretive methods see: Blaxter *et al.* (1996); Creswell (1994); Hakim (2000); Strauss and Corbin (1990).

## ASKING QUALITATIVE RESEARCH QUESTIONS: ESTABLISHING AIMS AND OBJECTIVES

In Chapters 3 and 5 we saw there are different ways in which research questions can be framed, and the two main styles involve the writing either of hypotheses or of aims and objectives. As the hypothesis was considered in the last chapter, the aims and objectives construction will be considered in this one. Of course, as noted in Chapter 5, although either style can be employed in a qualitative study, aims and objectives are more commonly used to set down the research question in an inductive qualitative study. You may, of course, be wishing to state a quantitative research problem using aims and objectives. This too is fine. Consequently, the example that will be used to demonstrate how to construct aims and objectives is taken from an actual research project. This project was commissioned as part of a policy evaluation by a government department in 1992 and undertaken by the author and four colleagues mentioned in the Acknowledgements. This project has been chosen as a suitable example as it involved triangulating both quantitative and qualitative methods.

In all honesty, most students are more comfortable working with aims and objectives than they are with hypotheses. One comes across aims and objectives in all areas of life – they are not limited to research. For example, if you picked up just about any basic textbook on public sector management you would probably find a section in it addressing the setting of organisational aims and objectives. In writing about the aims and objectives employed in the 1992 study McCulloch notes:

> The aims of the project are the broad descriptions of what you hope to achieve as a result of carrying it out.
>
> The objectives are more tightly-focused targets which, once achieved, will mean that you have attained the aims from which they are derived.
>
> The tasks are the individual activities which have to be undertaken in order to achieve the objectives.
>
> (McCulloch 1997: 7)

In other words, each step is logically derived from the previous one. Research aims are derived from the rationale of your research proposal, research objectives are derived from the aims and the tasks are in turn derived from the objectives. This is, again, an example of operationalisation, linking the theoretical with the empirical. Your aim will say something about the theoretical world, your list of tasks will focus upon the empirical investigations that you need to do and your objectives act as the link between the theoretical and empirical worlds. In this sense the objectives of a research project are similar to a hypothesis. If you find, however, that your tasks do not sit entirely within the confines of your objectives, or that your objectives do not sit entirely within the confines of your aims, etc. then something has gone wrong and you'll need to revise them. Aims, objectives and tasks should fit together like Russian dolls. If the smallest doll were to have a tail protruding from it for example, it would not fit. Look at Table 6.1 for an example of how one of the aims of the 1992 research project was broken down into objectives and tasks.

*Table 6.1* Aims, objectives and tasks

| | |
|---|---|
| *Aim* | To consider, in light of current government policy objectives for the environment and for the voluntary sector, how government resources may best be deployed in support of the voluntary sector in Scotland |
| *Objectives* | 1 To identify any overlaps and gaps in relation to public sector environmental policy objectives<br>2 To assess the topic areas and issues where the voluntary sector makes its most (and least) effective contribution |
| *Tasks* | 1 The examination of government documents on environmental policy<br>2 The examination of government documents on policy towards the voluntary sector<br>3 Interviews with Scottish Office officials concerned with relations with the Scottish voluntary sector<br>4 The development of indicators of the effectiveness of the contribution of the voluntary sector to the attainment of the government's environmental policy objectives |

*Source:* Based on McCulloch *et al.* (1993)

Thus, we see that in adopting the aims and objectives construction, thinking about what your tasks are will give you a clear steer as to what your methods need to be. In other words, construct validity will be added to your dissertation if your thinking progresses clearly and logically from topic → rationale → aims → objectives → tasks → method. Here again you can clearly see that the choice of method is primarily defined by the nature of the problem. As McCulloch has noted, 'Thinking about these things will improve your understanding of the issues involved in a project and will help you to unravel the logistics of the entire enterprise' (McCulloch 1997: 7). If you wish to read more about the setting of research aims and objectives however, please refer to Creswell (1994).

## METHODS FOR PRIMARY QUALITATIVE RESEARCH

In looking through the literature on qualitative research, you will commonly find reference to five main methods that can be used to gather primary data from the empirical world. These are: ethnography; participant observation; non-participant observation; unstructured interviews; and, group interviews (or focus groups as they are now often termed). Each of these qualitative methods is examined at closer quarters in due course. However, before you start to use any of these techniques, it is essential that you first make sure (whichever method it is you propose to use) that you take the time to get the people who you hope will participate in the study to agree to do so voluntarily.

In many ways this is more important than in the quantitative model. Remember that in qualitative research you investigate a smaller sample in greater depth. In essence, this means that where in a quantitative study you may involve yourself in a small way in the lives of many (e.g. asking a representative sample of a given population to complete a questionnaire) the opposite is normally the case in a qualitative piece of research. In other words, in undertaking qualitative research you will likely find yourself being involved in a more demanding way in the lives of a smaller number of people. Although non-participation is a problem in both quantitative and qualitative research, the problems associated with it are of a different order. For example, imagine that you are doing a quantitative dissertation and your response rate isn't quite what it should be. While this is not ideal, you may still be able to get some interesting findings from the data that you have managed to collect. On the other hand, if you have identified four key people you need assistance from to complete a piece of qualitative research and two of them refuse to help, it will be more than likely that you're going to have to go back to the drawing board. Whether this return to the drawing board will involve selecting new participants or whether it will involve a more radical rethink of the project as a whole will depend on the nature of your research problem and the data sought.

When approaching people to request their participation look back at the advice given in Chapter 2 on maximising voluntary participation. Whatever else you do, make sure that you do not lie to potential participants about what it is that you want of them (e.g. in terms of time, provision of documents, etc.). To engage in lying to potential participants would be wholly unethical and would in the long run, most likely end by causing you headaches when people withdraw their goodwill.

Blaxter et al. (1996) give good advice in noting that prior to approaching anyone for assistance with your research, you need to be absolutely certain that you have not only asked yourself the following questions, but that you have already formulated answers to them in your own mind.

1  Who or what do you want to research?
2  Who are the key individuals, or gatekeepers, from whom you need to get permission?
3  How much commitment will you require for your research from your subjects in terms of hours, days, weeks or months?
4  Is this reasonable?

5 Can you identify any potential problems with regard to
access?

(Blaxter *et al*.1996: 143)

Remember also, as noted in Chapter 2, that even where people
do give you an initial agreement to help in your research
endeavours they are of course, 'free to withdraw any offer of
assistance at any subsequent point'. Should such a misfortune
befall you, there is little that you can realistically do to remedy it
as, in the final analysis, 'Research is the art of the feasible'
(Blaxter *et al*.1996: 145). Thus, our attentions can now be turned
to the definition of the first three qualitative methods previously
mentioned: ethnography, participant observation and non-
participant observation. Definitions of these methods of primary
data collection are found in Table 6.2.

In considering the definitions in Table 6.2 you may not be
surprised to discover that these methods have their roots in
social subjects like anthropology and sociology. For example,
some readers may be acquainted with Pat Barker's recent trilogy
of historical novels *Regeneration* (now a feature film), *The Eye in the
Door* and *The Ghost Road* (Booker Prize Winner). One of the central
characters on both page and screen, Dr Rivers (1864–1922),
was a real man, in large part responsible for the early development of ethnographic methods. However, those acquainted with
Barker's work will also know that the type of anthropological
research in which Rivers was engaged has little in common with
the study of most modern political problems. Admittedly, such
methods *can* be used to address political questions and have in
fact enjoyed something of a renaissance in recent years in management research (you may therefore occasionally find reference
to ethnography, participant and non-participant observation in
the public administration literature). However, (as with the
warning issued about content analysis in Chapter 5), the author
would suggest that you only consider using these methods if

*Table 6.2* Definitions of ethnography, and participant and non-participant observation

| | |
|---|---|
| *Ethnography* | 'At its simplest, ethnography involves the researcher in describing the way of life of a group of people. Such a group may be large, as in the case of the community studies of whole towns, or quite small ... The purpose of such research is to describe the culture and life style of the group of people being studied in a way that is as faithful as possible to the way they see it themselves. The idea is not so much to seek causes and explanations ... but rather to "tell it like it is"' (McNeill 1990: 64–5). |
| *Participant observation* | 'participant observation is said to make no firm assumptions about what is important. Instead, the method encourages researchers to immerse themselves completely in the day-to-day activities of the people whom they are attempting to understand' (May 1997: 133). |
| *Non-participant observation* | The role of the non-participant observer, 'may be conceptualised as ... that of spectator in which the ethnographer only observes events and processes and thereby avoids becoming involved in interactions with subjects' (Gill and Johnson 1991: 109). |

you accept that their use relies upon fairly specialised techniques and that they are far more likely to be employed by a student of anthropology than a student of politics. Thus, to sum up this argument, if you already have an acquaintance with these techniques, an interest in using them and a problem that is amenable to being addressed through their application, by all means employ them to gather primary qualitative data. Assuming that appropriate supervision arrangements are also in place, you may find that you are able to produce a high quality and original undergraduate dissertation. If you do find yourself in this position, useful starting points for further reading include Schwartzman (1993) on ethnography and Jorgensen (1989) on participant and non-participant observation.

However, if not *all* of the four factors noted above (i.e. a suitable problem, appropriate supervision and an acquaintance with/interest in the techniques) are present, you may be best to give these methods a miss as the means of gathering primary data for an undergraduate dissertation in politics. As with content analysis, you can learn more about them at some future point. Thus, by a process of elimination, it is suggested here that the two means of gathering qualitative empirical information that will most likely be of relevance to the student of politics are the unstructured and group interview techniques.

While the unstructured (or 'depth') interview does share with the structured and semi-structured interviews the fact that it can be conducted either face to face or by telephone, there are not a great many other similarities between the quantitative and qualitative styles of interviewing. Consider the description of the unstructured interview reproduced below from Bouma and Atkinson:

> In general, qualitative research is associated with depth rather than width. This means that you will usually interview few people, but that the interviews will take some time; indeed they may be spread over several weeks, allowing you to reflect on what has gone before. The amount of time an interview takes will depend on the availability of the subject, but it is often a good idea to allow two or three hours so that the subject comes to feel at ease with you and you have time to follow up ideas – and indeed what might seem like irrelevances. You will not always know what is irrelevant until your research has pro-

gressed. You should try to build up a friendly relationship. This means that you should allow the interviewee to speak at his or her own speed and to talk about what interests them. Similarly you should try to avoid interrupting – this spoils the flow of speech. Omissions or points that are unclear can be sorted out later.

(Bouma and Atkinson 1995: 215)

It is plain to see why the qualitative one-on-one interview is described as the *unstructured* interview. What is being proposed in the above quotation is in some ways, more similar to an every-day conversation than it is to the structured quantitative interview in which a large number of respondents are asked a set of pre-determined questions in exactly the same order, using exactly the same wording each and every time. Indeed, many students of politics find that the unstructured qualitative interview is an excellent means of gathering their primary data. In the first instance, it is undoubtedly a more pleasurable experience to talk at length with a small number of respondents than it is to repeatedly go over the same questions with larger numbers of people with whom you form only a fleeting relationship. More importantly, however, it is a method that is suited to gathering information about the many political problems that do not easily lend themselves to quantification. For instance, if you wished to examine policy tensions between local and national party organisations, an unstructured interview with a small number of local politicians may prove the ideal method to use. Not only may the people concerned be wary of committing their thoughts to paper, but this is also truly a case where an inductive rather than a deductive approach may cast most light on the problem in hand. Every respondent will have their own personal views on national/local policy tensions and the easiest way in which to build a meaningful picture is to gather as much of this personal information as possible, without restricting the scope of the respondents to express their own point of view. You will, admittedly, have to try making sense of all this information when it comes to the data analysis stage, but this is simply part and parcel of the qualitative tradition. Data is gathered at an early stage and order is then imposed on the work through the analysis of that data, as clearly acknowledged by Bouma and Atkinson in the quotation above. One further issue that you ought to pay attention to regarding the unstructured interview – and you will find regular reference to it elsewhere – is the idea that 'Depth interviews are usually recorded and transcriptions of the tapes are generally analysed individually, although in the context of concepts and categories developed in the analysis of earlier interviews' (Walker 1985: 5).

Although such advice is the norm in the literature on unstructured interviewing, the author is going to suggest here that using a tape recorder can, as often as not, be counterproductive. In the first instance, be aware of the fact that most journalists, who essentially undertake (admittedly non-academic) unstructured interviewing on a daily basis, work with notebooks rather than tape recorders. Why do they do this? Writing from his own personal experience of unstructured interviewing, the author can only suggest that:

1 As soon as you switch a tape recorder on, the demeanour of many interviewees changes, as does the content of what it is that they have to say. You may find that they ask you to switch it off anyway if they are about to say something that is controversial. If on the other hand they don't ask you to switch it off, they may never say it.

2 You will find that transcribing tapes is a great idea if you have access to a skilled audio-typist. If you don't have access to such a person and to the specialist equipment that they use, you will find that it will take you roughly 8 hours to

transcribe every hour of tape that you've collected. Furthermore, in every hour of tape that you listen to there will be a lot of pauses, a lot of digression and a lot of passages that haven't recorded clearly because the interviewee had their head pointing away from the tape recorder for a minute. But if you feel that you do wish to use a tape recorder, don't transcribe the tapes – it will waste an enormous amount of your time to little avail. Better to let them play and take notes of the important material.

3 On a purely practical note, unless you can borrow a dictaphone, you may be unpleasantly surprised at the price of them.

Consequently, it is suggested here that the ideal means for making a record of unstructured interviews is the old-fashioned taking of notes. Although these notes will, of necessity, be brief, they should, if you write them up in full as soon as possible after the interview, serve as an accurate record. In most instances you can always check any queries with the interviewee afterwards.

As far as the second type of qualitative interviewing (the group interview or focus group) is concerned, the use of a tape recorder is even less worthwhile. Tapes made of such encounters, especially when more than one person is speaking at the same time, can be almost impossible to make sense of. Again, the taking of notes is commended to you as a means of making a record. Moreover, in terms of defining the group interview, Hakim notes that it involves a process where:

> between four and twelve people (eight being optimal) discuss the topic of concern for one or two hours with the guidance of a moderator. Focus groups produce less information on individual motivations and views than depth interviews can achieve, but they yield additional information as people react to

views they disagree with, or the group as a whole develops a
perspective on the subject.

(Hakim 2000: 35)

The author can only concur entirely with Hakim. In the first
instance, eight is an ideal number of people to have in a group.
Sometimes four people can be too small a number to create
much of a group dynamic and, if there is one dominant individual in such a small group, the others can be inclined to let
them take over. Twelve on the other hand is starting to get a bit
large. It can be difficult to keep track of everything that is being
said and it becomes easier for people who are of a quiet disposition to 'hide' in the larger group, saying very little or nothing. Hakim also hits the nail on the head when she notes that
there are certain types of information which will only be forthcoming in individual interviews and other pieces of information
that you will only get as a reaction to something that another
person has said in a group setting. Indeed, one often finds that
both methods are used in the same study to complement one
another.

A word of warning, however. It is almost certain that anyone
who is interested in British politics cannot fail to have heard of
the term 'focus group' given the fascination of the press for Tony
Blair's seeming near-dependence upon them as a means of gathering information to evaluate and influence policy direction. The
term 'focus group' has in fact started to take on something of a
pejorative meaning in the United Kingdom in recent times. Do
take care not to throw the baby out with the bath water when
assessing the merits of the group interview, though. The real
issue of concern regarding the use of focus groups in British
politics is not their value as a method of gathering primary
qualitative data, but is about the extent to which fickle public
opinion should drive policy in what has traditionally been a
representative democracy. Ultimately, though, if you do plan to

gather primary qualitative data through convening a group interview, bear in mind the following advice:

1 The role of the 'moderator', to use Hakim's terminology, is not the same as the role of the unstructured interviewer. There is undoubtedly a need in the group interview for the researcher to take at least a gentle lead in terms of directing and controlling the discussion. To do otherwise means that your agenda may well be overtaken by the agenda of the most forceful person in the group which frequently will not be entirely coterminous.

2 Although most sources that you will find in the literature advise against undertaking group interviews purely on grounds of efficiency, it would be foolish to deny that there are indeed efficiency gains to be had through the adoption of this approach. At the very least, if planning to mix a group interview with individual interviews, you will be able to cut down the number of individual interviews that you undertake and will therefore save yourself something in terms of time and costs of travel.

To sum up then, this section of the chapter has given a brief outline of the main methods of gathering primary qualitative data and the next section will be devoted to the use of secondary data sources. However, should readers be interested in finding out about collecting primary data using qualitative methods, they are directed towards the following sources: Blaxter *et al.* (1996); Bouma and Atkinson (1995); Bulmer (1984); Creswell (1994); Gilbert (1993); Hakim (2000); McNeill (1990); Marshall and Rossman (1999); Ragin (1994); Strauss and Corbin (1990); Walker (1985).

## ANALYSING SECONDARY DATA SOURCES

Two main types of qualitative research dependent upon second-ary data sources will be examined in this section – qualitative documentary analysis and the case study method. The first will only be addressed very briefly. In your degree studies so far, you will almost certainly have relied to a large extent on the qualita-tive interpretation of secondary sources as one of your main methods of both developing an advanced understanding of theoretical concerns and of introducing an empirical component to your essays, etc. Most readers will therefore already be skilled in qualitative documentary analysis and there seems little point in expanding at length on how to do it. If this book were aimed at, say, students of an experimental natural science, there might be merit in discussing the techniques required at length. How-ever, the author would indeed be surprised if there are many students of politics who have reached the stage of writing a dissertation without having mastered this skill. At this point, it is useful to refer readers back to Chapter 4 – specifically to the distinction that is drawn there between the literature review (establishing context, etc.) and documentary analysis (gathering data from printed sources). The main danger faced by a student undertaking a dissertation based upon the qualitative analysis of secondary data is that they produce little more than an outsize literature review. Thus, in undertaking such a piece of work, remind yourself from time to time of the distinctions that exist between the two types of working, despite the fact that both draw upon similar types of material. For instance, in a qualitative dissertation on British Labour Party Cabinets, you may wish to set out in a literature review general issues pertaining to British Cabinet Government and the Labour Party, in order that the reader of the dissertation becomes acquainted with the back-ground to the topic. Thereafter, however, you may choose to add an empirical component to the dissertation through, for example, focused qualitative analysis of documentary sources such as the published diaries of Tony Benn and Richard Crossman. To sum up, do not be misled by the brevity of this section regarding the importance of the role that can be played by qualitative documentary analysis in a dissertation that addresses a political problem with an empirical component. The section is purposely brief, as the author imagines that most readers are already competent practitioners of this method of research. If readers want further detail on how to undertake qualitative documentary analysis please refer to: Allan and Skinner (1991); Hakim (2000); May (1997); Preece (1994).

The second type of qualitative research dependent upon secondary data sources to be examined in this section is the case study. At the outset, there is a definitional/structural issue that needs to be addressed. The case study approach is the classic example of methodological triangulation. The approach actively encourages mixing and matching a variety of methods in the same study. Sometimes a case study may involve a mix of qualitative methods, sometimes a mix of quantitative and qualitative methods and it is not unreasonable to suggest that a piece of case study research could also rely upon a mixture of entirely quantitative methods. Moreover, case studies will regularly draw upon both primary and secondary data. Why then, has the case study method been fitted into this section of the book? Any author will be faced with a problem when trying to pigeonhole the case study approach, because simultaneously it fits in everywhere, yet nowhere. Thus, in this book, the decision was made to include the discussion of case studies within the qualitative chapter, as the approach focuses upon a small number of instances and investigates these instances in great depth. Furthermore, most case studies will rely to some extent on secondary sources of data, hence its inclusion here. Before moving on to define the case study further though, it is also worth noting that while case studies are often comparative exercises, they are not always so.

(Please refer to Chapter 7 for more information on the comparative method.)

In terms of definition, Blaxter *et al.* note simply that the case study approach involves, 'focusing your research project on a particular example or examples' (Blaxter *et al.* 1996: 54). This is as good a starting point as any other. In terms of defining a 'case', Hakim describes examples of cases thus: 'communities, social groups, organisations, events, life histories, families, work teams, roles or relationships' (Hakim 2000: 59). In other words then, a case used in a case study can basically be anything that you want it to be. Political parties could therefore be the basis for a case study, the local branches of political parties could be investigated using case study methods, the policies of political parties could form the basis of a case study dissertation, etc. Hakim notes:

> If surveys are the most multi-purpose of all research designs, case studies are probably the most flexible . . . The case study is the social research equivalent of the spotlight or the microscope: its value depends crucially on how well the study is focused. Case studies take as their subject one or more *selected* examples of a social entity . . . which are studied using a *variety* of data collection techniques. The criteria that inform the selection of the case, or cases, for a study determine its location on the continuum between the descriptive report as an illustrative example and the rigorous test of a well-defined thesis.
>
> (Hakim 2000: 59)

As far as the student of politics is concerned, in undertaking the research for their dissertation the case study approach is often ideal. The method itself encourages the adoption of the focused approach that is so central to the production of a good dissertation and allows you to draw your data from a wide variety of disparate sources (primary and secondary alike) using a variety of methods. As Blaxter *et al.* have noted, 'The case study is, in many ways, ideally suited to the needs and resources of the small-scale researcher. It allows, indeed endorses, a focus on just one example, or perhaps just two or three' (Blaxter *et al.* 1996: 66).

In choosing the *number* of cases that you will investigate, once again this is an issue of balance and judgement that will be informed by the very nature of your research problem itself. If you are unsure how many cases you should study, ask your dissertation tutor for advice. Certainly no more than the two or three mentioned by Blaxter *et al.* would be suitable for the undergraduate student producing a dissertation. Indeed (and this applies to all research designs, whether quantitative, qualitative or triangulated), there is an uncomfortable 'middle ground' that you should not stray into in terms of the number of instances that you study. For example, when somebody sets out to study twenty instances, they invariably get themselves into something of a mess, regardless of the method adopted. This number of instances cannot be studied in sufficient depth to produce a high standard of focused qualitative analysis, yet it is probably too small to be able to produce meaningful conclusions through statistical analysis. However, do remember that case study research, while often comparative, need not always be. A focus on a single case is often sufficient for the production of a high quality dissertation. For example, if you were to undertake a dissertation on social security fraud and within that topic chose to focus more specifically on housing benefit, you may find that little would be added to the study by comparing this problem with fraud involving the claiming of free prescriptions. Prescription fraud is usually carried out by people who do not have the few pounds that they need to pay for their medication. The most worrying type of housing benefit fraud, however, is carried out by corrupt but often wealthy landlords, who can claim thousands of pounds per month from the public purse for non-existent tenants. In this example, the motives for and scale of the activities that result in the state being defrauded are so dissimilar that there would be little point in conducting a comparative exercise. Better to stick with the single case study of housing benefit fraud and housing benefit fraud alone.

Moreover, if you bear in mind this warning about the number of instances that you choose to investigate, you will find that the case study approach lends itself well to the investigation of many of the 'messy' problems of social science. In effect, the case study approach involves the researcher in going right into the centre of Plate 2 and using all the techniques at their disposal to make sense of the mess that's to be found there. For these very reasons Yin, (an enthusiastic proponent of the case study approach), writes that:

> case studies continue to be used extensively in social science research – including the traditional disciplines (psychology, sociology, political science, anthropology, history, and economics) as well as practice-oriented fields such as urban planning, public administration, public policy, management science, social work, and education. The method also is a frequent mode of thesis and dissertation research in all of these disciplines and fields.
>
> (Yin 1994: xiii)

Thus, with more specific reference to the study of politics (and public administration/public policy) where so many of our problems are temporally and culturally bound, it is of particular relevance to cite Yin again. He notes, 'The case study is the method of choice when the phenomenon under study is not readily distinguishable from its context' (Yin 1994: 3). Consequently, the author commends to you the case study approach as wholly suitable to the investigation of a broad range of political problems, so many of which are not readily distinguishable from their context. To conclude this section, though, the author wishes to return to an example previously referred to in Chapter 2.

> Consider the researcher who wants to understand the fascination that some people have with guns – for example, gun collectors, some military personnel, hunters, and other enthusiasts. A big-picture view might show that certain categories of people (for example, lower middle-class white males) are more likely to collect guns and subscribe to magazines devoted to guns ... But does the big-picture view really say very much about the fascination with guns?
>
> (Ragin 1994: 81)

It may well be that the ideal way in which to address such a problem in a deep, meaningful and focused manner is through the application of the case study method.

For further reading about the case study approach you are directed towards two books – Stake's *The Art of Case Study Research* (1995) and Yin's *Case Study Research: Design and Methods* (1994) – both highly recommended sources.

## SUMMARY

From this chapter we may conclude:

1 that qualitative work is most often employed as a means of producing theoretical conclusions inductively, whether this be through the development of grounded theory or through suggestions for the modification of theory in light of empirical findings;

2 that qualitative work can be based on either aims and objectives or a hypothesis but that the former are commonly used;

3 that such aims and objectives, if clearly operationalised, provide both the structure for the planned qualitative piece of research and steer the student towards an appropriate choice of investigative methods;

4 that the student of politics is unlikely to be involved in gathering primary qualitative data though using methods such as ethnography, although there may be scope for the application of such methods in special circumstances;

5 that unstructured and group interviewing techniques may prove valuable to the student of politics in gathering primary data;

6 that a wide range of secondary sources are available to the student of politics who is engaged in researching and writing a dissertation;

7 that most students will already be acquainted with what is required of them in undertaking qualitative documentary analysis of secondary sources;

8 that the case study method is especially suited to the student of politics as many political problems are bound by temporal and/or cultural factors;

9 that the order tends to be imposed upon a piece of qualitative piece of work in the data analysis stage of the study; and

10 that, as discussed further in Chapter 8, data analysis in the qualitative tradition can prove problematic.

## TEST YOUR KNOWLEDGE OF THIS CHAPTER

Please refer to p. 19 for details.

# 7

## PUTTING THE CAT OUT

### The theoretical dissertation

## INTRODUCTION

With reference back to the plates at the begining of the book, the theoretical dissertation is one that does not make explicit reference to the problems of the empirical world that surrounds us. It does not address issues of cats messing up balls of wool. Rather, it is a dissertation that addresses, in depth, intellectual issues that have been identified from established theory. Theory is generated in the kingdom of the mind, as a simplified frame of reference to explain the incredibly complex and messy empirical political world that surrounds us. In discussing the theoretical dissertation, we are referring to a dissertation that is also firmly entrenched within the kingdom of the mind. There are of course a number of advantages to this style of working. For instance, although political theories are more or less always culturally and temporally bound to an extent, they are far less so than political issues which arise out of the empirical world. Consequently it is possible for instance to compare and contrast the Platonic view of human nature with the Marxist one. There would of course be far less point in comparing and contrasting the contemporary political issues of Plato's empirical world with those of Marx's empirical world. Indeed, if you think about it, the main reason that we still study the writings of Plato and Aristotle, and indeed the writings of those closer to us in terms of time and culture such as Bentham and Marx, is because of their theoretical value. None of these people discussed the politics of the modern welfare state. Thus, with reference to the plates and to the title of this chapter, doing a theoretical dissertation is very much about 'putting the cat out'. At the undergraduate level at least, it is about comparing and contrasting balls of wool *sans* cat.

The theoretical dissertation has already been mentioned a number of times in this book. In this way a few of its peculiarities have already been addressed. As a consequence, it makes sense here to review what has already been established about the theoretical dissertation and you will find below a synopsis of four main points:

1 In Chapter 1 a warning was issued concerning the attractiveness of the theoretical dissertation as an option: 'In such a study the focus could for instance involve comparing and contrasting photographs one and three on the plate, without regard to the empirical world. This is by no means an easy option for the dissertation student but is an option nonetheless.' Further explanation of this warning will be given in the next section of this chapter.

2 The example shown in Figure 3.1 (page 58) demonstrates how one may go about unpacking a problem for a theoretical dissertation. You may wish to refer back to Figure 3.1 at this stage. In looking at it again, you will note that getting started on a theoretical dissertation is not really much

different from getting started on any other dissertation. When unpacking your problem, however, you run the risk of straying away from the theoretical world and into the empirical world. If you find that your unpacking leads you away from those problems that truly belong to the kingdom of the mind, then you must ask yourself whether you are intending to do a theoretical dissertation after all. Remember, *all* academic dissertations will have a theoretical component. It is the extent to which dissertations address issues arising out of the empirical world that changes.

3  In Chapter 4 the following central distinction was drawn, '*do not fall into the common trap of confusing the dissertation that is based on literature review plus documentary analysis with the theoretical dissertation* . . . The theoretical dissertation is, admittedly, a dissertation based on literature review plus documentary analysis, but not all such dissertations are theoretical in nature.' The author has found that this is probably *the* commonest misconception about the theoretical dissertation (i.e. that a dissertation based on literature review and secondary sources is somehow 'theoretical'). While this distinction is a relatively straightforward one, the author has even worked alongside colleagues who confuse the theoretical dissertation with one which does not require the collection of primary data. Don't fall into this trap; remember the example given in Chapter 4 of the Australian student engaged in writing a dissertation on South African politics.

4  The fourth point that has been established (in Chapter 5) is that certain categories of hypotheses are particularly suitable for presenting the research problem in a theoretical dissertation and that (at the undergraduate level at least) it is best if such a hypothesis sets forth a problem amenable to solution through the adoption of the comparative method. Further explanation of the comparative approach will be given later in this chapter.

Thus, having reiterated these key points regarding the theoretical dissertation, we now proceed to examine in greater depth the warning issued in Chapter 1 and then briefly consider the comparative method and suggest why it is the most appropriate way for the undergraduate student of politics to proceed if undertaking a theoretical dissertation.

## POTENTIAL PITFALLS

Unfortunately, the simple fact of the matter is that many undergraduate students find that undertaking a purely theoretical dissertation proves less than fruitful. The main reason for this, is that in embarking upon a theoretical dissertation you are not taking the easy option. Consider a scenario in which a student meets with their dissertation tutor, states that they couldn't care less what their final dissertation mark is as long as the piece passes and asks for advice on how to do a dissertation that will scrape a minimum pass and nothing more. Thankfully the author can only comment on such a scenario in the abstract as he has never encountered it in the empirical world. The one piece of honest advice that the author could give to any student who is looking for an easy time of it, would be not to undertake a theoretical dissertation. There are five main potential pitfalls associated with the theoretical dissertation:

1 A good dissertation is one that stands out (naturally for positive rather than negative reasons). The two most obvious ways in which to make your dissertation stand out are to demonstrate to the examiner a well-developed, robust analysis of either an empirical issue or a theoretical one. In the author's opinion at least (and others may very well disagree), most dissertation students find it easier to make their work stand out by demonstrating a well-developed, robust analysis of an empirical issue than a theoretical one. This is

of course a generalisation. The converse is true for some students, but it is asserted here that these students are in the minority.

2 Bear in mind the advice offered in Chapter 3 regarding your own academic track record. Have your marks in theoretical classes been amongst your best? If so, then the theoretical dissertation may be the one for you. If not, then you might do better to think again about doing pure theory work. Moreover, even if you've had consistently good marks in theory classes, take care when selecting which area of theory it is that you wish to address in your dissertation. If you haven't read a good sample of the basic texts in the relevant area in the original already, get hold of them and look through them. It is a simple fact of life that some theoretical sources can be immensely complex. The material that is to be found in the lecture theatre and the textbook comes ready-digested by either your lecturer or the author. Bear in mind that it may have taken them years or even decades of study to be able to unravel sources that can be truly arcane to the uninitiated. That said, you can also find that reading sources in their original is sometimes easier than ploughing through enormous quantities of secondary analysis. For instance, if anyone wishes to understand Thomas Kuhn's *The Structure of Scientific Revolutions* (1970) it is far easier to read the original book than it is to read the masses of secondary comment on it. In similar vein, the plethora of confused and confusing secondary sources that were published in his own lifetime reportedly led Marx to assert that he was 'not a Marxist'.

3 There is a danger in the theoretical dissertation of 'losing' the focus. There is not the same emphasis on having to perform certain tasks in a structured order to gather this and that piece of empirical information that will be needed before you can draw conclusions about your chosen problem. If the focus becomes lost the theoretical dissertation can

end up looking a bit like nothing more than a large literature review.

4　Remember there is a danger of getting drawn too far into the empirical world if you are not careful in the planning and execution of the theoretical dissertation. If this happens you may end up with a dissertation that is neither one thing nor the other, which addresses neither the theoretical nor the empirical in sufficient depth. Once again, this is an issue of maintaining your focus. If you can maintain your focus this problem should not occur.

5　Finally, although it may seem a trivial question, are there any instrumental reasons that may come into play in your deciding whether or not to do a theoretical dissertation? If you have set your heart on a particular career path, you may be well advised to do a dissertation related to such a career – one that you can then wax lyrically about in job interviews. That said, if you haven't decided exactly what it is that you want to do, if your chosen career path is one of the many that do not require you to have a particular degree or if your ideal career is in academia, then doing a theoretical piece of work may be an enjoyable and worthwhile activity. Indeed, you may never have the opportunity to undertake a serious piece of theoretical work again. There are few opportunities to engage in such pursuits in most lines of work.

If you have read and considered this list of potential pitfalls and still think that the theoretical dissertation is something that you want to do, speak to your dissertation tutor and, if they are in agreement, go for it. The intention in this chapter is not to say that nobody should do theoretical dissertations, far from it. Rather, the intention is to suggest that it may not prove the ideal choice for everyone. The author is (he, at least, thinks) one of those people who believes that diversity in educational experiences is every bit as central to the survival of a robust civilisation as biodiversity is to the survival of robust ecosystems. Today we live in an age, it sometimes seems, of rampant instrumentalism. For instance, it is now the case that '40 per cent of all Scottish undergraduates are studying business-related degrees' (Kerevan 2001: 7). The author is personally hopeful that the theoretical dissertation will remain a vital part of the diversity of higher education. The nub of the issue, though, is whether you and your dissertation tutor are agreed that a theoretical piece of work is right for you. If so, then go for it.

## THE COMPARATIVE METHOD

Having considered the potential pitfalls associated with the theoretical dissertation we are now truly ready to 'put the cat out'. Thus in this section a brief explanation of the comparative method will be given. No pretence is made that this chapter contains anything like a full review of the comparative method. You will no doubt be aware that the study of comparative politics and comparative government is an enormous sub-field in its own right. You may even be studying for a degree in comparative politics, in which case there will, in all honesty, be little of interest to you here. Of course, as was noted in Chapters 5 and 6, the comparative method's usefulness is by no means limited to comparison of theoretical issues; it can be very usefully applied in addressing the problems of the empirical world too. Nevertheless, it will be suggested that in the *undergraduate theoretical dissertation* at least, comparison is best considered an almost essential feature. This is the main reason behind the inclusion of discussion of the comparative method in this, rather than any other chapter.

As suggested in Chapter 1 and further reiterated here, the theoretical undergraduate dissertation most often involves the comparison of two (or perhaps three, but bear in mind the comment in Chapter 6 about spreading your efforts too thinly) theoretical stances. Look back, for instance, at both the plates and at Figure 3.1, both of which propose a comparison of two theories. This does not, however, mean that comparing two or three theories is the only way in which theoretical work can be undertaken, far from it. Rather, the suggestion here is that in trying to compare more than two or three theoretical stances you will, within the scope available in an undergraduate dissertation, be unable to do full justice to them all.

It is also possible to do theoretical work that consists mainly of a focused criticism of *a single* theoretical stance. However, quickly look back to Chapter 1 where comment was passed about the relative rarity of people who can coherently write down their world-view in a manner that is free from contradictions. There is a similar scarcity of people who can, from first principles, work out a new angle on questions of political theory. Indeed, if this were such an easy task, the ideas of Plato, Aristotle, Bentham and Marx may well by now be largely redundant – historical curios overtaken by a raft of new theoretical perspectives. This of course is not the case at all. It would be an extremely tall order even for a PhD student to embark upon such a task and the author would find it hard to believe that anyone would recommend such a course of action to an undergraduate. Developing 'an original contribution to knowledge' is the litmus test of the doctoral degree, not the undergraduate degree. Thus, if you harbour ambitions to develop new theoretical perspectives of your own, keep them at bay at least until you've finished your dissertation and your undergraduate degree. Once again, bear in mind that you have the rest of your life to devote to making an original contribution to knowledge.

As noted earlier the comparative approach to the study of politics and government is an enormous sub-field in its own right. *The Concise Oxford Dictionary of Politics* (Mclean 1996) notes that comparative government is, 'One of the main subdivisions of the study of politics'. We saw earlier that the use of the comparative method is by no means restricted to theoretical comparison. If the truth is told, theoretical comparison is a far less commonly practised activity than comparison of the empirical. You might be surprised to read that one of the most common criticisms of the application of the comparative method in the past was that empirical comparisons were being drawn without due regard to theory. But here we are with the proposition that such an approach be used to compare and contrast theoretical perspectives.

The reason for this is quite simple. Basically, comparative politics has in the past focused mainly upon issues that have arisen from the empirical world. If, for example you pick up any basic textbook on the subject, e.g. Blondel's *Comparative Government: An Introduction* (1995), you will probably find a wealth of material on empirical investigative techniques such as: the behavioural approach to comparative politics; comparative analysis of the dynamics of structures; comparative analysis of political systems (classifications approach); the institutional approach to comparative government, etc. This material is simply a reflection of the way in which the field has developed. There is nothing to say that comparative methods cannot also be applied usefully in considering theoretical issues. Although it is probably the area of comparative method about which the least has been written, you can find materials on the *conceptual approach*, which takes as its subject matter for comparison values, principles, ideologies etc. Of all that has been written on the comparative method, it is the material on the conceptual approach that will be of value in thinking about how to conduct a comparative criticism of two or more theoretical stances.

If you are reading this section because you contemplate employing comparative analysis in addressing an empirical rather than a theoretical issue, you may find the literature to be a double-edged sword. On the one hand, so much more has been written about empirical comparisons that it is very easy to find material. On the other hand, you could find that so much has been written about empirical comparison that it becomes confusing. To repeat, the comparative approach to the study of politics is an enormous sub-field in its own right and a wealth of literature exists. Thus, this section ends with the provision of a (very) basic list of sources to which you can refer initially regarding the comparative method: Blondel (1988, 1995); Hague et al. (1998); Landman (2000); Macridis and Brown (1990); Marsh and Stoker (1995); Pennings et al. (1999).

## SUMMARY

From this chapter we may conclude:

1 that the theoretical dissertation addresses intellectual issues that have been identified from established theory;
2 that political theories are in general culturally and temporally bound to a lesser extent than political issues which arise from the empirical world;
3 that in choosing to do a theoretical dissertation you are not embarking on an easy option;
4 that it can be less easy to maintain focus in undertaking a purely theoretical dissertation than in one that contains an empirical component;
5 that the theoretical dissertation should not address more than two (or at the very most three) theoretical positions;
6 that great care needs to be taken in deciding which areas of theory are to be addressed within the dissertation;
7 that attempting to develop theoretical advances is not a realistic goal of an undergraduate dissertation (although structured and critical comparison is);
8 that the comparative approach has traditionally been used principally to address problems arising in the empirical world;

9  that the comparative approach does however have merit in addressing theoretical problems; and

10  that both student and tutor need to be satisfied that the theoretical dissertation will be of good quality.

## TEST YOUR KNOWLEDGE OF THIS CHAPTER

Please refer to p. 19 for details.

# 8

## MAKING SENSE OF IT ALL

### Critical thought and data analysis

### INTRODUCTION

In this chapter the emphasis will be on the application of critical and balanced judgement to the analysis of the data that you have collected. At the outset, in terms of defining quantitative and qualitative analysis, it is first worthwhile reminding ourselves of the key distinctions between the two kinds of research model. These key distinctions will impact upon the way in which we analyse our data every bit as much as they did on the way we gathered it. As Blaxter *et al.* (1996) note:

> Quantitative research is, as the term suggests, concerned with the collection and analysis of data in numeric form. It tends to emphasise relatively large-scale and representative sets of data, and is often, falsely in our view, presented or perceived as being about the gathering of 'facts'. Qualitative research, on the other

hand, is concerned with collecting and analysing information in as many forms, chiefly non-numeric, as possible. It tends to focus on exploring, in as much detail as possible, smaller numbers of instances or examples which are seen as being interesting or illuminating, and aims to achieve 'depth' rather than 'breadth'.

(Blaxter *et al.* 1996: 60)

The differences in style of working give rise to differences in style of data analysis (although both will involve balanced critical judgement). Babbie's definitions of the two analytical styles are reproduced for you below:

*quantitative analysis* – The numerical representation and manipulation of observations for the purpose of describing and explaining the phenomena that those observations reflect.

*qualitative analysis* – The nonnumerical examination and interpretation of observations, for the purpose of discovering underlying meanings and patterns of relationships.

(Babbie 1995: glossary)

Data analyses in the quantitative and qualitative models of research are different, yet they are underpinned by similar key practical considerations. The similarities in terms of the key practical issues to which due consideration must be given to produce a good quality dissertation, are summarised in these four paragraphs:

1 You need to set aside an adequate period of time in which to analyse your data. It is not uncommon for students to continue reviewing literature and gathering data as the deadline for their dissertation's submission looms up. This can be particularly problematic if your work relates to a fast-moving and topical problem. However, it is an unfortunate

fact of life that any dissertation can only address issues as they are up to some point in time – otherwise the end would never come. In law dissertations for instance, it is required of students that they state the date up to which their consideration of the law is valid. In other words, the passing of judgement in a case or the passage of a new piece of legislation can render the student's dissertation outmoded even before it is examined. There is no way round this sort of problem, it is part and parcel of life and you just have to live with it. The point in the process must inevitably come when you have to say to yourself 'Enough'. It is not profitable to gather more and more data if you do not have time to analyse it properly. It is always a sad sight to come across masses of data tucked away in an appendix to the dissertation that has obviously been back-breaking to gather but which has not been properly ana-lysed. It is after all what you do with your data that is of the greatest significance, not how much or how recently it was gathered.

2 Assuming that you have allowed yourself sufficient time for your data analysis, you need to ensure thoroughness, whether your dissertation is based on quantitative or quali-tative data. The key here is to try to work methodically through your data, ensuring that no stone remains unturned by repeatedly asking questions of both data and yourself, e.g. could this be related to that? If you manage to complete your data analysis and manage to draw some con-clusions from the analysis at a sufficiently early date, pass the material on to your dissertation tutor and ask them to check what you've done. In this way you can either rest easy or address any shortcomings as a result of the feedback received.

3 The third similarity between quantitative and qualitative analysis of data is that both are reliant upon the exercise of

critical and balanced judgement on the part of the dissertation student.

4 Regardless of whether your dissertation is based upon quantitative or qualitative data, conclusions based on flawed analysis of that data will at best be regarded as weak, at worst as nonsense.

Thus, there are a number of key similarities between quantitative and qualitative data analysis – there are, of course, differences too. In the quantitative study we impose order upon our work at an early stage through an elongated planning period, and are then usually in a position to collect and analyse our data relatively quickly. Indeed, analysis in quantitative research can now be done very quickly indeed, thanks to the proliferation of powerful computerised packages for the analysis of quantitative data. The key to successful quantitative data analysis, as noted in Chapter 5, is not so much the ability to apply statistical tests as the ability to decide which tests are appropriate to use – and certainly those which are not.

Within the qualitative study order tends to be imposed upon our work at a later stage, through an elongated period of data analysis. Consequently, if you are undertaking a qualitative piece of work, you really do have to ensure that you leave yourself plenty of time to sort out and make sense of the data that you've gathered.

The remainder of this chapter will be given over to reinforcing the idea that whichever the mode of data analysis, be it quantitative or qualitative, it will require the exercise of balanced critical judgement. As previously asserted, this is not a book about statistical testing, nor is it a book about the a, b, c of interpreting qualitative information. There is already a wealth of material available on both types of analysis. You will find that just about any basic book on social scientific research methods will provide you with a fuller description of how to analyse qualitative data. Similarly, if you are planning to undertake quantitative analysis, there is no shortage of source material available and more or less any basic book on statistics will be of use to you. Further reading has been listed at the end of this chapter to help you. Here we want to press home the need for critical and balanced judgement in the data analysis stage of the dissertation, as invariably in the social sciences, such judgement will need to be invoked:

> Because observations in the real world seldom if ever match our expectations perfectly, we must decide whether the match is close enough to consider the hypothesis confirmed. Put differently, can we conclude that the hypothesis describes the general pattern that exists, granting some variations in real life?
>
> (Babbie 1995: 54)

## QUANTITATIVE DATA ANALYSIS

Note that the quotation above relates to both quantitative and qualitative data analysis. There is a danger in undertaking quantitative analysis of assuming that because quantitative data analysis techniques are precise, this means that the conclusions that can be drawn from such analyses are also precise. This is not so. In Chapter 5 the distinction was drawn between deterministic and probabilistic conclusions. In the study of empirical political problems we deal in probabilistic conclusions and, as a consequence, answers that are often far from precise. Thus, precision in procedure does not imply precision in answer – hence the need for the exercise of judgement in quantitative analysis. In the deductive model of quantitative empirical research at least, we are most often engaged at the analytical stage in the testing of hypotheses, with a view to drawing some conclusions regarding the explanatory adequacy of the original theoretical starting point from which the study derived. As noted earlier, the advent of computer packages for statistical testing has made this task very much easier (assuming that you've identified the most appropriate test to apply).

While not wishing to advocate particular packages, it would be foolish to ignore the fact that there are two market leaders with which you are probably acquainted – SPSS and MiniTab. Until recently these packages were something of a nightmare to use. Analysing quantitative data involved typing in a line command every time you wanted the computer to do something. However, with the advent of Windows-driven systems, the user-interface has become far friendlier in the latest releases and – as with all Windows-driven packages – once you've got the hang of the basics, you can find your way around them quite easily. You will almost certainly find that your institution has made either SPSS or MiniTab available for you to use (probably both) and both are recommended. This is not to suggest that there are no other excellent products available in the marketplace, merely to acknowledge the dominance of these two. Nevertheless, regardless of the detailed nature of the statistical tests to be employed and regardless of whether these tests are to be performed by hand or through the use of computer packages, we must ensure when undertaking quantitative analysis that we address at the very least the following three questions:

1 *Are our results representative?* If your quantitative data are from a representative sample then you will be able to generalise, i.e. the findings from the sample analysis will also be applicable to the whole population from which the sample was drawn. Low response rates, etc. can often jeopardise representativeness. If, as a consequence of non-response, etc. you are left with an unrepresentative sample, it is not the end of the world. Although not ideal, all that this means is that you cannot generalise from them, but you can still draw valid conclusions about the data that you *have* managed to gather.

2 *Are the tests that we're proposing to undertake suited to our data?* Refer back to Chapter 5 for further explanation of this point.
3 *To what level of confidence are we working?* Commonly in the social sciences we work to either the 95 per cent or the 99 per cent level of confidence. We are rarely confident about our findings to the 99.9 per cent level.

'What is a confidence level?', the author hears some of you ask. Ackroyd and Hughes note, 'there is a choice about the level of accuracy we want to accept. Confidence limits of 95 per cent and 99 per cent are conventionally used in most statistical calculations in social research' (Ackroyd and Hughes 1992: 72). So, confidence levels are to do with the accuracy of our quantitative findings. Basically, because in a quantitative study we are involved in searching for patterns in large sets of data, there is always a likelihood that some of the patterns that we observe are simply an artefact of chance. For example, in a class of thirty children there is some chance that two or more, will share the same birthday. (The *probability* of two identical birthdays is about 0.006, if we assume random births. This is fairly small – but coincidences do happen.) Adopting strict confidence levels is about trying to account for the effects of chance in creating patterns in data sets. Having a 95 per cent level of confidence means that we can be 95 per cent confident that a real relationship exists between two variables. By the same token however, in adopting a 95 per cent level of confidence we are acknowledging that there is a 5 per cent chance that no real relationship exists between the variables, and that the pattern observed in the data is merely a random coincidence. In the natural sciences researchers tend to work with confidence levels of 99 or 99.9 per cent but in the social sciences we tend to work with confidence levels of 95 or 99 per cent. In so far as dissertation research is concerned, the 95 per cent level of confidence will nearly always suffice. If confused about the issue of confidence levels, check the further reading at the end of the chapter. If you are unsure whether the 95 per cent level of confidence is appropriate for your work, check with your dissertation tutor.

Thus, there is undoubtedly precision built into the processes of quantitative data analysis in that:

- there are given ways to establish whether you can generalise from your findings;
- there are clearly established ways in which statistical tests should be applied to data; and
- there are means of establishing that relationships between variables are not simply a reflection of chance.

Unfortunately, however, there is less precision involved in the drawing of meaningful conclusions for your dissertation. It is not enough for you to simply point to an appendix containing masses of statistical output and suggest that the dissertation's conclusions are to be found therein. In much the same way as the quantification of data can involve the translation of essentially non-numerical information into a numerical format (as described in Chapter 5), in drawing conclusions you will be required to turn your statistical output back into plain English (or whatever language your dissertation is to be submitted in).

It is at this stage in the analysis of quantitative data that you will be required to exercise balanced critical judgement. For instance, it is possible to gather data in a systematic way, analyse it using the best procedures available and then discover unusual or unexpected findings from this analysis. You might for example, find an interesting link between two variables during data analysis that you had not anticipated at all.

Even assuming that your work has been imbued with sufficient construct validity during the processes of operationalisation and writing the research proposal, weird patterns can present themselves to you during data analysis. In such a case immediately adopt a *critical* stance. Interesting as the finding may be, is it central or extraneous to the purpose of your dissertation? If it is extraneous (and many of these types of finding are), simply record in your dissertation the fact that you have made the finding, suggest that it may be interesting to follow it up further in the future and note that it cannot however be investigated any further at this point in time. Do not go off and draw conclusions about some finding that is extraneous to the purpose of your dissertation. To do so undermines the good work that you have done to date. Treat data critically, you cannot use them all.

Within the quantitative model then, the process of turning statistical output into conclusions is largely one of judgement. At the end of the day, even assuming that you present conclusions that are wholly consistent with your purpose, remember to do so in a balanced and justified manner. Working in this way will leave your conclusions less open to attack. Moreover, bear in mind that in drawing conclusions about political problems (even quantitative ones) we are nearly always drawing conclusions that are essentially probabilistic rather than deterministic in nature. Whatever you do then, avoid bold assertions to the effect that your work has 'proved' this that and the other. Far better to err on the side of caution and suggest that your findings are supportive of the initial theoretical proposition.

To sum up this section, remember we saw in Chapter 5 that, quantitative data are fallible. Think back to the example of the newspaper report headlined 'Sensational result of *People* poll . . . DIANA *WAS* MURDERED! 98% believe plot killed Di and Dodi'. Interpretation of numerical information always requires the application of critical and balanced judgement on the part of the dissertation student. Statistics is not an exact science. As Babbie warns, 'Ultimately, then, scientists use imperfect indicators of theoretical concepts to discover imperfect associations' (Babbie 1995: 77).

## QUALITATIVE DATA ANALYSIS

Qualitative interpretation is in large part personal interpretation – but not *too* personal. Your analysis must not appear to the examiner to be lacking in critical and balanced judgement. Data analysis is the stage in the research process that is likely to cause the dissertation student the most difficulty. This is because, unlike the precise nature of many quantitative procedures, there is not just one 'right' way of doing qualitative analysis. This is not entirely a bad thing of course as the idea after all is that you bring your own personal interpretation to bear on the analysis of the data in hand. A cursory review of the literature does, however, provide *hints* on how to analyse qualitative data. For instance, Creswell notes that:

> Several components might comprise the discussion about the plan for analysing the data. The process of data analysis is *eclectic*; there is no 'right way' . . . Metaphors and analogies are as appropriate as open-ended questions. Data analysis requires that the researcher be comfortable with developing categories and making comparisons and contrasts. It also requires that the researcher be open to possibilities and see contrary or alternative explanations for the findings. Also the tendency is for beginning researchers to collect much more information than they can manage or reduce to a meaningful analysis.
>
> (Creswell 1994: 153)

Similarly, Strauss and Corbin, ardent proponents of the qualitative method, refer to the problems of qualitative data analysis in the preface to their 1990 volume:

> This book is addressed to researchers in various disciplines (social science and professional) who are interested in inductively building theory, through the qualitative analysis of data.

However exciting may be their experiences while gathering data, there comes a time when the data must be analysed. Often researchers are perplexed by this necessary task. They are dismayed not only by the sheer number of fieldnote, document or interview pages ('mountains of data') now confronting them, but are often troubled by the following questions. How can I make sense out of all this material? How can I have a theoretical interpretation while still grounding it in the empirical reality reflected by my materials? How can I make sure that my data and interpretations are valid and reliable? How do I break through the inevitable biases, prejudices, and stereotypical perspectives that I bring with me to the analytic situation? How do I pull all of my analysis together to create a concise theoretical formulation of the area under study?

(Strauss and Corbin 1990: 7)

If you are to overcome the problems noted by Strauss and Corbin, the one thing that is important above all else in the analysis of qualitative data is the need to fit that data into categories. All of your data cannot be analysed at the same time. The human brain just cannot cope. Thus, you will need to assign the data to logical groupings before you can start to interpret its meaning. This is what is meant by imposing *order* on the qualitative study through the process of data analysis. The development of analytical categories and the 'coding' of data (i.e. deciding which category a certain piece of information is to be assigned to for analysis) are necessary prerequisites to analysis itself. Neither the development of categories nor the coding of qualitative data is easy, and as so often the case in the qualitative tradition, there is no agreed procedure for doing these things. The best advice the author can offer the student who is engaged in such an activity is as follows:

1 Ensure that your analytical categories are consistent with the aims and objectives of your dissertation. If they're not, you won't be able to draw valid conclusions.

2 In developing categories, there is a fine balance to be struck between developing too few (as noted above, you cannot analyse all of your data at once) and developing too many (which may result in you losing oversight of the problem and lead to work that lacks coherence). If in doubt, use the dissertation's objectives as categories.

3 Once you have developed your analytic categories, get your dissertation tutor to quickly reconcile these with your original aims and objectives.

4 Code your data critically. When working with qualitative information it can sometimes be difficult to decide how to code it, as data may fit into more than one category. Admittedly it is easier to analyse the data if you can fit each piece of information into a single category, but this will not always be possible. Do not therefore 'force' information into only one category unless it seems appropriate to do so. As ever, the category to which you assign a given piece of information will depend upon critical and balanced judgement.

Finally, the best sources of reference available to you on the tricky business of data analysis for the qualitative dissertation are Creswell (1994) and Strauss and Corbin (1990). However, these sources will not provide you with answers – only hints. Remember that if ever there was a need for reliance upon your own skills of criticism and judgement, doing qualitative data analysis is it.

For further reading on data analysis more generally, refer to some of the following: Ackroyd and Hughes (1992); Anderson (1989); Babbie (1995); Black (1993); Blaxter et al. (1996); Booth (1992); Creswell (1994); Fitz-Gibbon and Morris (1987); Gilbert (1993); Huff (1954); Kapadia and Anderson

(1987); Kinnear and Gray (1994); Marshall and Rossman (1999); Moser and Kalton (1971); Pennings, *et al.* (1999); Preece (1994); de Vaus (1996).

## SUMMARY

From this chapter we may conclude:

1 that in four key practical ways, quantitative and qualitative data are similar;
2 that in the analysis of quantitative data account must be taken of whether the data concerned is representative;
3 that the analysis of quantitative data must rely on tests that are suited to the data in hand;
4 that the issue of confidence levels must be addressed when analysing quantitative data;
5 that statistical findings must be translated back into a linguistic form in the dissertation's conclusions;
6 that qualitative analysis is eclectic;
7 that despite the above, qualitative analysis *does* require the dissertation student to generate categories for analysis;
8 that the student must 'code' the qualitative data into appropriate categories;
9 that the conclusions of the qualitative dissertation are drawn out of the analytic categories, with reference to the original aims and objectives; and
10 that both quantitative and qualitative data analysis are dependent upon the exercise of critical and balanced judgement on the part of the dissertation student.

## TEST YOUR KNOWLEDGE OF THIS CHAPTER

Please refer to p. 19 for details.

# 9

## MAKING SENSE OF IT ALL

### Drafting, completing and submitting the dissertation

Once you've finished your data analysis you are ready to produce the final draft of your dissertation. The ways in which
people like to work differ so, by the time that students have
finished their analysis, different people will be at different stages
in their writing up. This does not matter particularly although
what does matter is that by the *end* of the drafting process you
have a piece of work that is near-complete. The one thing that
you must try your very best to do is to get your final draft completed as far in advance of the submission date as possible. When
academic staff are faced with a draft dissertation the day before
submission is due, there is little meaningful that they can do to
comment upon it. It is not the dissertation tutor's responsibility

when a draft is handed in. Meaningful feedback can be given to those students who hand their drafts in early but not to those who hand drafts in at the last minute. Handing work in early to your dissertation tutor for checking is for your benefit not theirs.

However, before you hand a final draft in to your tutor for checking, go through the draft one last time and subject it to a critical appraisal. If your draft does not adequately address each of the six points set out below it is not a final draft:

1 Does your writing demonstrate that you have understood the conceptual range and complexity of the chosen topic?
2 Does your writing demonstrate that you are aware of the literature available on the topic and have assessed the issues and opinions arising from that literature in a manner which is appropriate to the area of investigation?
3 Does your writing demonstrate that you have chosen and used appropriate research methods?
4 Does your writing demonstrate that you have collected, analysed and assessed data which are relevant to the area of investigation?
5 Does your writing demonstrate that you have brought a critical and balanced point of view to bear upon the evidence gathered?
6 Does your writing demonstrate that you have drawn conclusions based on a balanced discussion of the evidence?

Once you have received feedback on your final draft, considered it carefully and made amendments accordingly. You are now ready to complete the dissertation. Completion is essentially a fairly technical stage, where you address matters such as layout and style. In a completed dissertation students are expected to organise and display their findings in a clear and coherent manner, to demonstrate high editorial standards and to present their work in a consistent manner throughout. Does your work match up? The only way to check is to subject it to careful proof reading, a slow, laborious but nevertheless absolutely essential task. A typographical error can, in some instances, seriously compromise the integrity of a sentence without it necessarily being apparent to the reader that the error concerned is indeed typographical in nature.

Once you've proof read your work, add the following parts to the dissertation if you haven't already done so: title page; abstract; acknowledgements; and, list of contents. Appendices should also be paginated and included at this stage. As far as the title page is concerned, it is especially important to get this right. The title page is, after all, the first thing that an examiner will see. Your own institution will almost certainly have its own guidelines on the information that a title page should contain and your dissertation tutor should be able to help you locate this. But if you are free to design it in your own way, it is customary to place the following information on a title page:

- the full title of the dissertation;
- the full name of the author;
- the award for which the dissertation is submitted;
- the name of the degree awarding body;
- the year of submission.

You are now ready to get your work bound and to submit it. As far as binding is concerned, your institution may have regulations regarding the form of binding to be used. If it does, follow them to the letter. Even if it doesn't, make sure that you choose something that is suitably sturdy as your work may be read by a number of examiners and it is important that it remains in one piece. You are advised to ask your dissertation tutor how many copies you are to submit and make sure that you keep an identical one for your own reference. The dissertation must be submitted on time. Once it is submitted as a finished piece of work the copyright in the work will (nearly always) remain vested in yourself as the author of an unpublished work. Now all you have to do is wait and see whether all your hard work has paid off.

To conclude the book the author can only state his hope that you will find the process of writing your dissertation in politics a fruitful and worthwhile exercise, in both intellectual and personal terms. Remember that the dissertation is a piece of work that will stay with you for the rest of your life and consequently it is worth pulling out all the stops and giving it your all. Bear in mind that some of the advice offered in this book might contradict advice that you have been given in your own institution. If so, stick with the advice that you are offered locally as there is no unique way in which to do a dissertation. At the end of the day, all that is contained here is suggestion. Make full use of your dissertation tutors throughout the process, but do not hound them. When you do consult them it is useful not only to have thought through what it is that you want to speak about but to have examples of the issues that you want to address written down on paper. The last sentence of this book will give you the best piece of advice of all. *Although advice should never be taken lightly, no matter what you have read in this book and elsewhere and no matter what advice you are given by staff in your own institution, all final decisions regarding your dissertation are for you and you alone.*

# BIBLIOGRAPHY

Ackroyd, S. and Hughes, J. (1992) *Data Collection in Context*, 2nd edn, London: Longman.

Allan, G. and Skinner, C. (eds) (1991) *Handbook for Research Students in the Social Sciences*, London: Falmer.

American Political Science Association Committee on Professional Ethics, Rights and Freedoms (1991) *A Guide to Professional Ethics in Political Science*, 2nd edn, Washington DC: American Political Science Association.

Anderson, A. (1989) *Interpreting Data: A First Course in Statistics*, London: Chapman and Hall.

Ayer, A. (1990) *Language, Truth and Logic*, 2nd edn, Harmondsworth: Penguin.

Babbie, E. (1995) *The Practice of Social Research* 7th edn, Belmont: Wadsworth.

Bath Information and Data Services (2001) *BIDS: Providing Bibliographic Services for the UK Higher Education and Research Community*. Online. Available HTTP: <http://www.bids.ac.uk/> (accessed January 2001).

Bell, J. (1999) *Doing Your Research Project: A Guide for First-Time Researchers in Education and Social Science*, 3rd edn, Buckingham: Open University Press.

Bergström, S. (1993) 'Value Standards in Sub-Sustainable Development: On Limits of Ecological Economics', *Ecological Economics* 7, 1: 1–18.

Black, T. (1993) *Evaluating Social Science Research: An Introduction*, London: Sage.

Blaxter, L., Hughes, C. and Tight, M. (1996) *How to Research*, Buckingham: Open University Press.

Blondel, J. (ed.) (1988) *Cabinets in Western Europe*, Basingstoke: Macmillan.

Blondel, J. (1995) *Comparative Government: An Introduction* 2nd edn, London: Prentice-Hall/Wheatsheaf.

Bookchin, M. (1990) *The Philosophy of Social Ecology: Essays on Dialectical Naturalism*, Montréal: Black Rose.

Booth, D. (1992) *A First Course in Statistics*, 2nd edn, London: DP Publications.

Bouma, G. and Atkinson, G. (1995) *A Handbook of Social Science Research: A Comprehensive and Practical Guide for Students*, 2nd edn, Oxford: Oxford University Press.

Bulmer, M. (ed.) (1984) *Sociological Research Methods: An Introduction*, 2nd edn, Basingstoke: Macmillan.

Campbell, T. (1981) *Seven Theories of Human Society*, Oxford: Clarendon.

Chalmers, A. (1982) *What is This Thing Called Science?*, 2nd edn, Milton Keynes: Open University Press.

Creswell, J. (1994) *Research Design: Qualitative and Quantitative Approaches*, Thousand Oaks CA: Sage.

Cryer, P. (2000) *The Research Student's Guide to Success*, 2nd edn, Buckingham: Open University Press.

Cuba, L. and Cocking, J. (1994) *How to Write About the Social Sciences*, London: HarperCollins.

Doyal, L. and Harris, R. (1986) *Empiricism, Explanation and Rationality: An Introduction to the Philosophy of the Social Sciences*, London: Routledge.

Durkheim, E. (1964) *The Rules of Sociological Method*, 8th edn, London: The Free Press of Glencoe.

Editorial (1997) 'Diana Was Murdered: 98% Believe Plot Killed Di and Dodi', *The People*, 9 November: 1–7.

Evans, K. (1984) *Planning Small Scale Research*, 3rd edn, Windsor: NFER-Nelson.

Feyerabend, P. (1975) *Against Method: An Outline of an Anarchistic Theory of Knowledge*, London: New Left Books.

Fitz-Gibbon, C. and Morris, L. (1987) *How to Analyze Data*, Newbury Park CA: Sage.

Frisby, D. and Sayer, D. (1986) *Society*, Chichester: Ellis Horwood.

Giddens, A. (1971) *Capitalism and Modern Social Theory: An Analysis of the Writings of Marx, Durkheim and Weber*, Cambridge: Cambridge University Press.

Gilbert, N. (ed.) (1993) *Researching Social Life*, London: Sage.

Gill, J. and Johnson P. (1991) *Research Methods for Managers*, London: Paul Chapman.

Hague, R., Harrop, M. and Breslin, S. (1998) *Comparative Government and Politics: An Introduction*, 4th edn, London: Macmillan.

Hakim, C. (2000) *Research Design: Strategies and Choices in the Design of Social Research*, 2nd edn, London: Routledge.

Homan, R. (1991) *The Ethics of Social Research*, London: Longman.

Huff, D. (1954) *How to Lie With Statistics*, Harmondsworth: Penguin.

Hughes, J. and Sharrock, W. (1997) *The Philosophy of Social Research* 3rd edn, London: Longman.

Jones, B., Gray, A., Kavanagh, D., Moran, M., Norton, P. and Seldon, A. (1998) *Politics UK* 3rd edn, Hemel Hempstead, Prentice Hall.

Jorgensen, D. (1989) *Participant Observation: A Methodology for Human Studies*, Newbury Park CA: Sage.

Kapadia, R. and Anderson, G. (1987) *Statistics Explained: Basic Concepts and Methods*, Chichester: Ellis Horwood.

Keat, R. and Urry, J. (1975) *Social Theory as Science*, London: Routledge and Kegan Paul.

Kerevan, G. (2001) 'What Became of the Plate Glass Revolution?', *The Scotsman Education*, 24 January: 7–9.

Kimmel, A. (1988) *Ethics and Values in Applied Social Research*, Newbury Park CA: Sage.

Kinnear, P. and Gray, C. (1994) *SPSS for Windows Made Simple*, Hove: Psychology Press.

Kuhn T. (1970) *The Structure of Scientific Revolutions* 2nd edn, London: University of Chicago Press.

Landman, T. (2000) *Issues and Methods in Comparative Politics: An Introduction*, London: Routledge.

McCulloch, A. (1997) *Learning Paper 10: Preparing a Research Proposal*, Aberdeen: The Robert Gordon University.

McCulloch, A., Baxter, S., Moxen, J., Macleod, C., Mackay, M. and Silbergh, D. (1993) *An Assessment of The Scottish Office Environment Department's Contribution to the Voluntary Environmental Sector*, Aberdeen: The Robert Gordon University.

McLean, I. (ed.) (1996) *The Concise Oxford Dictionary of Politics*, Oxford: Oxford University Press.

McNeill, P. (1990) *Research Methods*, 2nd edn, London: Routledge.

Macridis, R. and Brown, B. (1990) *Comparative Politics: Notes and Readings*, 7th edn, Pacific Grove: Brooks/Cole.

Magee, B. (1982) *Popper*, 2nd edn, London: Fontana.

Marsh, D. and Stoker, G. (eds) (1995) *Theory and Methods in Political Science*, Basingstoke: Macmillan.

Marshall C. and Rossman, G. (1999) *Designing Qualitative Research*, 3rd edn, Thousand Oaks CA: Sage.

May, T. (1997) *Social Research: Issues, Methods and Processes*, 2nd edn, Buckingham: Open University Press.

Moser, C. and Kalton, G. (1971) *Survey Methods in Social Investigation*, 2nd edn, Aldershot: Dartmouth Publishing.

Papineau, D. (1978) *For Science in the Social Sciences*, Basingstoke: Macmillan.

Parkin, F. (1982) *Max Weber*, London: Routledge.

Pennings, P., Keman, H. and Kleinnijenhuis, J. (1999) *Doing Research in Political Science: An Introduction to Comparative Methods and Statistics*, London: Sage.

Pettigrew, T. (1996) *How to Think Like a Social Scientist*, New York: HarperCollins.

Popper, K. (1969) *Conjectures and Refutations: The Growth of Scientific Knowledge*, 3rd edn, London: Routledge and Kegan Paul.

Popper, K. (1980) *The Logic of Scientific Discovery*, 4th edn, London: Hutchinson.

Preece, R. (1994) *Starting Research: An Introduction to Academic Research and Dissertation Writing*, London: Pinter.

Punch, M. (1986) *The Politics and Ethics of Fieldwork*, Newbury Park CA: Sage.

Ragin, C. (1994) *Constructing Social Research: The Unity and Diversity of Method*, Thousand Oaks CA: Pine Forge Press.

Rudestam, K. and Newton, R. (2000) *Surviving Your Dissertation: A*

*Comprehensive Guide to Content and Process*, 2nd edn, London: Sage.

Russell, B. (1912) *The Problems of Philosophy*, London: Oxford University Press.

Saunders, M., Lewis, P. and Thornhill, A. (1997) *Research Methods for Business Students*, London: Pitman.

Schwartzman, H. (1993) *Ethnography in Organisations*, Newbury Park CA: Sage.

Scottish Tourist Board Planning and Development Division (1993) *Standardised Questions for Tourism Surveys*, 2nd edn, Edinburgh: Scottish Tourist Board.

Sieber, J. (1992) *Planning Ethically Responsible Research: A Guide for Students and Internal Review Boards*, Newbury Park CA: Sage.

Stake, R. (1995) *The Art of Case Study Research*, Thousand Oaks CA: Sage.

Strauss, A. and Corbin, J. (1990) *Basics of Qualitative Research*, Newbury Park CA: Sage.

Sykes, J. (ed.) (1982) *The Concise Oxford Dictionary of Current English*, 7th edn, Oxford: Oxford University Press.

Trigg, R. (1985) *Understanding Social Science: A Philosophical Introduction to the Social Sciences*, Oxford: Blackwell.

UK Data Archive (2001) *UK Data Archive*. Online. Available HTTP: <http://www.data-archive.ac.uk/> ( accessed 29 January 2001).

University of Surrey (2001) *The Question Bank: Social Surveys and Research Questionnaires Online*. Online. Available HTTP: <http://qb.soc.surrey.ac.uk/> (accessed 19 January 2001).

de Vaus, D. (1996) *Surveys in Social Research*, 4th edn, London: University College London Press.

Walker, R. (ed.) (1985) *Applied Qualitative Research*, Aldershot: Gower.

Weber, R. (1990) *Basic Content Analysis*, 2nd edn, London: Sage.

Yin, R. (1994) *Case Study Research: Design and Methods*, 2nd edn, Thousand Oaks CA: Sage.

# INDEX